TRANSFORM TRAUMA

Live The Life You Love

DENISE RANE

Contents

Introduction

What if the life you love isn't a distant dream... but a truth waiting within you?

You've survived. That's already a miracle.
But you were meant for more than survival.

In *Transform Trauma – Live the Life You Love Living*, author and fellow survivor [Your Name] offers a healing invitation—a pathway from the invisible weight of trauma into a life filled with possibility, joy, and purpose.

Written by someone who has walked this road herself, this compassionate and powerful guide meets you right where you are. Through personal stories, gentle guidance, and practical tools—including emotional intelligence, growth mindset, body awareness, forgiveness, and more—this book becomes a companion, not a prescription.

It's time to lay down what's not yours to carry.

It's time to return to yourself.

You've carried the weight of trauma long enough. It's time to transform it.

CHAPTER 1
Putting Down the Invisible Cloak

*"You don't have to carry the weight
of your past to prove how strong you are."*

— Unknown

The Morning Weight of Shadows

Imagine waking up each morning with something heavy pressing against your chest. This isn't a physical weight you can see or touch— it's deeper and quieter. It's the invisible cloak woven from fear, shame, silence, and grief. You stir from sleep, hoping the new day might bring relief, but that familiar heaviness lingers.

It's as if the emotions, memories, and unmet needs of yesterday wrap around you before your feet even hit the floor. If this resonates, you're not alone. That cloak—the one no one else can see but you carry every day—is one of the most common side effects of surviving trauma.

Acknowledging this cloak is the first brave step toward transformation.

Understanding the Invisible Cloak

Trauma doesn't always scream; it often whispers. It embeds itself in the pauses between conversations, the fear behind your smile, or the voice in your head that says, "You're too much," or "You're not enough." This cloak forms in layers—woven from experiences that taught you it wasn't safe to speak up, feel deeply, or be fully seen.

When you've worn this cloak for years, it can feel like part of you. But it's not. It's something that was placed on you—by abuse, neglect, betrayal, or fear. While you didn't choose it, you do have the power to start removing it. Not all at once, not perfectly—but piece by piece, gently and intentionally.

The Science of Trauma's Impact: How Trauma Affects Your Brain

Trauma doesn't just affect your thoughts; it shapes your brain and nervous system in ways that can feel invisible yet powerful. When we experience overwhelming events, especially in childhood, our brain adapts to keep us safe. These adaptations often become part of the "invisible cloak" we carry.

A key part of the brain involved is the **amygdala**, your emotional alarm system. After trauma, the amygdala can become hyperactive, constantly scanning for danger—even when you're safe. This leads to a heightened stress response, making you feel on edge, anxious, or easily overwhelmed.

Meanwhile, the **prefrontal cortex**—responsible for rational thinking and emotional regulation—can become underactive during distress, making it hard to feel grounded or make decisions. The **hippocampus**, which helps process and store memories, may encode trauma as fragmented and disjointed, resulting in flashbacks or emotional flooding.

But here's the good news: your brain is capable of change. Through **neuroplasticity**, you can gently rewire these responses. Practices like breathwork, grounding, journaling, mindfulness, and therapy help re-engage the prefrontal cortex and calm the amygdala. Over time, your brain learns that it's safe to release the cloak and to live without the constant burden of hypervigilance or shame.

You are not broken. You are rewiring. Every act of self-care, reflection, and courage signals to your nervous system that safety and healing are possible.

The Cost of Carrying the Cloak

Bearing an invisible cloak of trauma impacts more than just your emotions—it influences every aspect of your being.

- Chronic Stress: When you're constantly anticipating danger or rejection, your nervous system stays in survival mode. This drains your energy, disrupts your sleep, and can lead to burnout or physical illness.
- Difficulty Trusting Others: If betrayal or violation shaped your past, your cloak may compel you to keep others at a distance. Even safe relationships can feel threatening.
- Lack of Energy or Passion: Continuously managing hidden pain can dull your sense of joy. Dreams get postponed, and life becomes more about coping than thriving.
- Self-Doubt and Shame: You may question your worth, your voice, or whether your healing even matters. This inner dialogue isn't your truth—it's the cloak speaking.

Recognizing these effects helps validate why you may feel exhausted or stuck—and why releasing just one thread of the cloak can transform everything.

Shedding the Heavy Cloak

To embark on the journey of transformation, you must first acknowledge what you're carrying.

Ask yourself:

- Where does the weight manifest in my life?
- In relationships that drain me?
- In the way I speak to myself?
- In the dreams I keep postponing?

Start by taking an honest inventory. Identify the areas where you feel heavy. Notice how you navigate your day. Journaling, working with a trauma-informed coach or therapist, or exploring somatic tools like breathwork can help you uncover the "threads" of your cloak—and begin to loosen them.

Letting go won't happen overnight. But every thread you name is one you begin to unravel.

What Keeps the Cloak in Place?

If the cloak is so burdensome, why do we cling to it? The answer lies in what the cloak has protected us from—pain, vulnerability, or the unknown. Over time, we internalize beliefs that keep the cloak tightly fastened:

- "If I let go, I'll forget what happened."
- "I don't deserve to feel better."
- "This pain is part of who I am."

These beliefs may have been necessary once, but they no longer serve you. Gently questioning them can shift your perspective. Ask yourself: Who would I be without this belief? What freedom could I embrace if I didn't need to carry this anymore?

You are allowed to release what was never yours to bear in the first place.

My Truth: The Day I Said, "I'm Tired"

There was a time when I didn't even realize I was carrying anything. I thought I was just "too sensitive," "not strong enough," or that something was wrong with me. I minimized my pain, told myself others had it worse, and tried harder to fit in and hold it all together. I didn't see the cloak—I just felt the weight.

Then one early morning, I went for a walk. The world was still sleeping, and mist hung in the air like the fog I felt inside my chest. I stopped, took a shaky breath, and whispered out loud: "I'm tired."

That tiny moment was everything. It wasn't dramatic or loud, but it was honest. For the first time, I admitted the truth—not just to myself but to the universe.

And something shifted.

That sentence became a thread I could pull on. I didn't drop the whole cloak in one day, but that was the first thread. And that was enough.

If you've ever whispered your own version of "I'm tired," know this: it's not weakness. It's a beginning.

Stories of Overcoming

Take Maya, for instance—a public speaker and advocate who once lived in silence. She spent years hiding her pain behind a successful career and a bright smile, but inside, she bore her own invisible cloak. It wasn't until she allowed herself to speak—first to herself, then to others—that her life began to change. Sharing her story helped her breathe again and enabled others to see that they weren't alone.

Stories like Maya's (and mine, and yours) reveal something vital: healing doesn't have to look like a breakthrough moment on a stage. Sometimes it manifests as a whisper in the dark, a deep breath, or a single step toward your truth.

Reader Spotlight: Lila's First Thread

Lila had been in therapy for years. She understood the science of trauma, could name her attachment style, and had read all the books. Yet, something still felt stuck.

Then one day, her therapist posed a new question: "What would happen if you stopped proving your pain?"

Lila paused and cried. That afternoon, she wrote in her journal: "I don't need to keep wearing my suffering to honor what I've survived."

That became her first thread.

She didn't discard the cloak. Instead, she folded a piece of it gently and placed it on her altar. Then she took a walk, just like I did. For the first time, she felt the sun touch her back, not just her burden.

Her healing began not in knowing—but in feeling.

Empowerment and New Beginnings

Now, return to your own mornings.

What if the light streaming through the window didn't just reveal the weight of yesterday—but illuminated the possibilities of today? What if the story you've been telling yourself could shift—from survival to empowerment, from burden to becoming?

Understanding your cloak is not weakness—it's wisdom. Naming it requires courage. And letting go, even a little, is liberation.

Try This Tool: Morning Grounding Practice

Each morning, take 3–5 minutes to check in with yourself. Before reaching for your phone or to-do list, place your hand over your heart and breathe deeply.

Ask yourself:

- What am I carrying that isn't mine?
- What does my body feel like it needs today?

Visualize setting down that invisible cloak—even just for a moment. Imagine yourself standing lighter, more open, and more present.

Repeat this for a week and journal any changes you notice in your mood, body, or breath.

Bonus Practice: The Power of Naming

Take a quiet moment to name specific memories, phrases, or beliefs that still feel tied to your cloak.

- "You're too much."
- "You should be over this by now."

- "You always mess things up."

Write them down on small slips of paper. For each one, ask: Is this mine to keep? If not, tear it up or burn it safely. Feel the shift. Each name you assign to the pain is a step toward releasing it.

Naming brings clarity. And clarity brings freedom.

Guided Visualization: Laying Down the Cloak

Find a quiet space. Close your eyes and take three deep, grounding breaths.

Now picture yourself standing in a soft, dim forest. A heavy cloak is wrapped around your shoulders. What color is it? What is the texture? Feel the weight pressing against your back and heart.

Now, with great care, reach for the clasp. Unfasten it gently. Let the cloak fall to the forest floor.

As you stand there—bare, real, and whole—feel the breeze against your skin. Imagine warmth and sunlight touching parts of you long hidden.

Say to yourself: "I am safe to let this go. I am allowed to be free."

Stay in this moment for as long as you need.

This visualization can be repeated daily or whenever the weight returns.

Reflective Workbook Page: Chapter 1

Reflection Questions:

1. What are you carrying that doesn't belong to you?
2. How does this cloak affect your relationships, dreams, or self-worth?
3. What might it look or feel like to begin removing one thread of that cloak?

Journal Prompts:

- Write about a moment when you realized something from your past still held you back.
- Describe what your "invisible cloak" is made of—what beliefs, fears, or experiences have woven it?
- Imagine a day without the cloak. What might feel different in your body, mind, or spirit?

Affirmation:

"I acknowledge the weight I carry and honor my courage to begin letting it go."

Flowing Forward

Now that you've identified the weight you've been carrying, your next step is to understand your emotional world. In the next chapter, we'll explore how emotional intelligence helps you navigate your feelings with courage and clarity.

CHAPTER 2
Building Emotional Intelligence

"When awareness is brought to an emotion, power is brought to your life."

— Tara Meyer Robson

The Overwhelming Tide

In the heart of a bustling city, you sit in a café, nursing a cup of cold coffee. Outside, the world rushes by, but inside, your mind is a whirlwind of exhausting, chaotic emotions. It all started with a single oversight at work, snowballing into a day where everything unraveled. Frustration quickly escalated into anxiety, crashing over you without warning. As your thoughts spiral, it becomes clear that understanding and managing these emotions requires more than mere endurance; it calls for emotional intelligence.

Many trauma survivors navigate their days with an emotional barometer set to "overwhelm." It's not just the current challenge—it's the accumulation of past hurts, unspoken needs, and internalized pressure. Emotional intelligence doesn't mean you're never triggered; it means you know how to meet the trigger with self-awareness instead of shame.

Embracing Emotional Intelligence

Emotional intelligence serves as your vessel through the turbulent waters of feelings and interpersonal dynamics. This skill not only aids in understanding your emotions but also shapes how you respond to others, communicate, and recover from emotional storms.

The five core components of emotional intelligence are:

- Self-awareness – Recognizing your emotions as they arise.
- Self-regulation – Managing those emotions in healthy, constructive ways.
- Motivation – Channeling emotional energy toward positive outcomes.
- Empathy – Understanding and sharing the feelings of others.
- Social skills – Building meaningful connections through communication and trust.

Together, these elements create a foundation for grounded, emotionally rich relationships—with yourself and with others.

When you can name your feelings, regulate your responses, stay connected to your goals, and respond to others with care, you begin to feel empowered in your life—not just reactive.

The Science of Emotional Intelligence: How Your Brain Supports Growth

Emotional intelligence isn't just a feel-good concept; it's grounded in neuroscience and psychology. Researchers like Daniel Goleman, who popularized the term, describe emotional intelligence as involving both the prefrontal cortex (responsible for decision-making and self-awareness) and the amygdala (which triggers emotional responses like fear or anger).

When we practice emotional intelligence—especially self-awareness and regulation—we begin to reshape these brain circuits through a process called neuroplasticity. This is your brain's ability to form new pathways and responses over time, proving that healing is not just possible; it's biological.

For many trauma survivors, the amygdala can become overactive, putting the nervous system in a constant state of alert. Emotional intelligence practices—like mindful breathing, journaling, and naming emotions—help calm this response and strengthen the brain's ability to respond with presence rather than panic.

Studies support this shift. In a 2010 study published in Psychological Science, participants who labeled their emotions (e.g., "I feel anxious") showed decreased amygdala activity and increased regulation from the prefrontal cortex. This means that every time you pause and identify what you're feeling, you're rewiring your brain for resilience.

By practicing these skills, you're not only improving your emotional world but also fostering better decision-making, deeper relationships, and improved health outcomes, such as reduced stress hormones and increased immune function.

Expanding Your Emotional Vocabulary

Sometimes, emotional overwhelm arises not from the feeling itself but from a lack of words to describe it. When all emotions are labeled as "bad," "too much," or "wrong," we lose the nuance and power that emotional intelligence can offer.

Start by building your emotional vocabulary. Go beyond "happy," "sad," "mad," and "anxious." Try words like:

- Frustrated, discouraged, overwhelmed, hopeful
- Peaceful, uncertain, empowered, disconnected
- Curious, embarrassed, grateful, lonely

The more specific your words, the more accurately your brain and body can respond. This isn't just semantics; it's strategy. Emotional granularity (naming emotions with precision) is associated with improved emotional regulation, reduced depression, and greater resilience.

When you give your emotions language, you empower yourself.

Charting the Course

The journey begins with self-awareness. This is your internal compass, helping you notice your reactions before they dictate your behavior.

- Keep a journal to track emotional patterns.
- Practice mindful breathing when emotions feel intense.
- Name your feelings aloud when you feel safe to do so.

From awareness grows self-regulation—your ability to stay steady in the storm. This doesn't mean suppressing emotion; it means responding thoughtfully.

- Take a pause before reacting.
- Choose your words with intention.
- Learn to soothe your nervous system through grounding practices.

Motivation empowers you to keep going, even when things are hard. It's that inner fire that reminds you your healing is worth the effort.

- Set small goals that align with your values.
- Celebrate emotional wins—like staying present in a difficult moment.

Empathy is where emotional intelligence fosters connection. By stepping into others' perspectives, you deepen relationships and grow your own compassion.

- Listen fully before offering advice.
- Reflect back what you've heard to build trust.

Finally, social skills translate emotional insight into relational success.

- Practice assertive communication.
- Express appreciation often.
- Repair misunderstandings with honesty.

These skills may not come naturally, but they can be practiced, refined, and integrated. Emotional intelligence is not a trait you either have or don't; it's a muscle you build.

My Truth: Emotions as Strength, Not Weakness

I used to think emotional intelligence meant not crying in front of others or staying calm during conflict. But in truth, I was stuffing things down, ignoring my needs, and believing that being "emotionally strong" meant hiding pain.

Once, during a heated conversation with someone I loved, I paused. Instead of shutting down or lashing out, I said, "I feel really hurt right now, and I need a moment." That was new for me—and it changed everything.

The moment I learned to name my feelings—fear, shame, joy, hope—I began to find power in honesty. I stopped trying to perform calmness and started practicing genuine emotional connection. That changed everything. I felt less alone and more like myself.

If you've ever felt that your emotions are "too much" or that they've made you weak, know this: your feelings are valid, and learning to work with them is one of the most courageous things you can do.

Journeys of Resilience

Consider Alex, a survivor who transformed his chaotic emotional landscape into a symphony of balance and grace. Through daily practice, he began responding rather than reacting. His leadership blossomed, as did his relationships.

Jane, a poet and speaker, became known for her empathy and clarity. But her growth didn't happen overnight—it bloomed from years of tuning into her emotional world and aligning her words with her truth. Her resilience became her rhythm, and her authenticity became her anchor.

These stories illustrate that emotional intelligence isn't about perfection; it's about presence. It's learning to stay with yourself, even when things feel difficult.

Embrace the Power Within

Back in that café, with your coffee and chaotic thoughts, imagine taking a breath. Instead of trying to fix everything, you pause. You name the feeling: "I'm overwhelmed." You place a hand on your chest and say, "And that's okay."

That's emotional intelligence in motion.

Let self-awareness guide you. Let regulation protect you. Let motivation carry you. Let empathy expand you. Let your social skills connect you.

You are already worthy—and these tools can help you live as if that's true.

As you continue this journey of self-discovery, your next step is just as important: shifting the mindset that shapes how you see the world—and yourself. Let's explore how beliefs can either keep you stuck or set you free.

Try This Tool: The Name-It-to-Tame-It Exercise

At least once a day, pause and identify what you're feeling.

- "I feel anxious."
- "I feel hopeful."
- "I feel overwhelmed."

Then add: "And that's okay."

This practice helps you regulate emotional responses by creating space between your feelings and your reactions. It teaches your brain that you are safe to feel—and builds self-trust, one emotion at a time.

Reflective Workbook Page: Chapter 2

Reflection Questions:

1. When was the last time you paused to ask yourself what you were really feeling, not just what you were thinking?
2. Given your current challenges, which area of emotional intelligence (self-awareness, regulation, motivation, empathy, or social skills) feels most nourishing to develop?
3. How might your relationships shift if you expressed your emotions with more clarity, curiosity, and compassion?

Journal Prompts:

- •Describe a time when your emotions felt overwhelming. What was hiding beneath the surface?
- Write about a moment when empathy—either given or received—helped change a conversation, a conflict, or a connection.
- Reflect on the messages you received about emotions growing up. Which ones are you ready to release? What would you like to replace them with?

Affirmation:

"I honor my emotions as guides, not enemies. I grow stronger each time I choose to feel and respond with intention."

Flowing Forward

With your emotional awareness expanding, we'll now turn inward to the thoughts that shape your reality. Let's explore how mindset can unlock new possibilities and rewrite old narratives.

CHAPTER 3
Shifting Your Mindset

"Whether you think you can,
or you think you can't—you're right."

— Henry Ford

Breaking Free from the Chains of Limiting Beliefs

Imagine standing in the middle of a dense forest, striving to reach the open sky, yet constantly pulled down by unseen vines—woven from self-doubt, fear, and shame. These aren't just fleeting thoughts; they're deeply rooted beliefs formed during times of survival. Phrases like "I'm not enough," "I'll never change," or "Someone like me doesn't get to dream" echo in your mind.

These thoughts feel familiar, making them all the more convincing. But what if they aren't the truth? What if they're merely remnants of the past, holding you back from the life you're meant to create?

This chapter invites you to begin loosening those vines and lifting your gaze to the possibilities above. A new story—one grounded in growth, courage, and self-trust—can become your reality.

The Transformative Power of Mindset

Mindset is the lens through which you interpret the world—and yourself. It shapes how you approach failure, receive feedback, and perceive possibility.

Cultivating a growth mindset means:

- Viewing failure as part of learning.
- Embracing effort as essential to progress.
- Trusting in your capacity to evolve.

Where a fixed mindset declares, "I've reached my limit," a growth mindset asserts, "I'm still becoming." By shifting this lens, you begin to reclaim authorship over your life. You're not stuck—you're evolving.

Navigating the Currents of Change

Mindset isn't just a belief—it's a practice. It's something you return to, moment after moment.

- Notice limiting beliefs. Listen for phrases like "I'm just not good at this" or "That's not for me."
- Question the familiar. Ask, "Is this belief true—or just an echo of the past?"
- Reframe with compassion. Replace "I'm failing" with "I'm learning."

Each time you make this shift, you gently rewire your brain. With repetition, the familiar becomes flexible, and the stuck places soften.

To strengthen a growth mindset:

- Surround yourself with people who believe in growth.

- Celebrate progress, not perfection.
- Reflect often. Acknowledge the inner work that goes unseen.

The Science of Mindset: How Beliefs Rewire the Brain

Your brain is not fixed—it's adaptable. Through a process called **neuroplasticity**, your thoughts and beliefs shape the structure and function of your brain over time. Repeated thoughts create stronger neural pathways, meaning the more you think "I can grow," the more natural growth becomes.

When you challenge old beliefs and replace them with empowering ones, you engage your **prefrontal cortex**, responsible for planning, decision-making, and forward-thinking. This area strengthens with every moment of reflection, every reframe, and every choice to believe in your potential.

Simultaneously, the **amygdala**, sensitive to threat, begins to calm down. Shifting your mindset teaches your brain that trying something new doesn't mean danger—it means expansion.

Functional MRI studies reveal that individuals who practice growth-mindset thinking are more resilient in the face of failure, more persistent in their efforts, and even perform better under pressure. The act of believing in yourself changes your biology, not just your perspective.

So every time you say, "I'm learning," "I'm growing," or "I choose to see possibility," you are not just affirming hope—you're rewiring your life.

My Truth: I Am Not Broken. I Am Becoming.

For a long time, I believed my worth was defined by my past. I thought my story was too messy, too damaged, too far gone. I carried the belief that I had to remain small, quiet, or hidden.

But then I began reading stories of others who had risen. I listened to mentors and participated in retreats that helped me see myself in a new light. One day, in a quiet moment, I wrote in my journal: "I am not broken. I am becoming."

That shift—subtle yet profound—began to unravel years of inner doubt. I didn't suddenly become confident or fearless, but I did become willing. Willing to question the narrative. Willing to take up space. Willing to stop seeking permission to grow.

Each time I challenged a limiting belief—whether about my intelligence, healing, or voice—I was building new muscles. I started saying yes to things I once thought were "for other people." I allowed myself to be seen. I applied for roles I felt underqualified for. I shared my story with trusted individuals.

And here's what I learned: Growth doesn't require perfection. It only demands participation.

You don't have to believe it all at once. But even a crack in the armor of doubt lets the light in.

Mindset and Identity: Reclaiming Who You Really Are

Your mindset doesn't just shape how you think—it shapes who you believe you are. For many survivors, trauma distorts identity. We internalized not just fear, but false identities: I'm too sensitive. I'm hard to love. I'm not enough.

But mindset empowers you to rewrite the script.

When you change how you think, you begin to change how you see yourself. You're not the broken person your trauma depicted. You are the one brave enough to keep showing up, wise enough to ask deeper questions, and worthy of building a life rooted in truth, not fear.

Try asking yourself:

- Who do I want to believe I am becoming?
- What if I stopped identifying with pain—and started identifying with possibility?
- How would I show up if I believed I am already enough?

This isn't about denial—it's about redesign. You're not erasing the past; you're choosing what defines you moving forward.

Let your mindset become a mirror—reflecting your wholeness, not your wounds.

Survivor Spotlight: Elijah

- Core struggle: Believed he would always be stuck in survival mode
- Turning point: Daily journaling revealed how harsh his inner voice had become
- Ongoing practice/tool: Weekly belief audits and affirmations
- Where they are now: Mentors young adults and leads mindset workshops

Survivor Spotlight: Renee

- Core struggle: Avoided trying new things for fear of failure

- Turning point: Took a painting class and discovered joy in imperfection
- Ongoing practice/tool: Journals her "proof pages" of growth
- Where they are now: Hosts art-based healing workshops and speaks on creative courage

Reshape Your World

Imagine walking back into that forest. This time, you recognize every limiting belief as just a vine—tangled, yes, but no longer unmovable. One by one, you begin to untwist them. With each thread released, your posture shifts. You grow taller. You begin to see the sky.

Mindset is the foundation from which your new life will rise. Not a perfect life—but a powerful one. One where your past doesn't dictate your future.

Try This Tool: Limiting Belief Reframe

Write down three thoughts that regularly hold you back. They might sound like:

- "I'll never be confident."
- "No one will understand me."
- "I always mess things up."

Now rewrite each one as a growth-minded truth:

- "I'm learning to speak with confidence."
- "The right people will value my truth."
- "Every mistake helps me improve."

Practice reading these aloud daily. Allow your brain to start believing a new story.

Reflective Workbook Page: Chapter 3

Reflection Questions:

1. What is one limiting belief you've carried that no longer serves you?
2. When did you last surprise yourself by doing something you didn't think you could?
3. If your mindset shaped your reality, how might your life change if you believed you were enough as you are?

Journal Prompts:

- Write a letter to a younger version of yourself who believed they weren't enough. What do you want them to know now?
- Make a list of "I can't..." statements and rewrite each one into an "I'm learning to..." belief.
- Reflect on an obstacle you once thought would break you—but instead taught you something valuable. What did you learn?

Affirmation:

"I release the beliefs that no longer serve me and embrace the power to grow, change, and rise."

Flowing Forward

Now that you've begun to challenge limiting beliefs and reclaim your mindset, it's time to explore the deeper work of emotional release and self-compassion. In the next chapter, we'll examine forgiveness—not as a gift to those who hurt you, but as a way to free yourself and reclaim your power.

CHAPTER 4
The Power of Forgiveness

"Forgiveness is not about letting someone off the hook for their actions, but freeing yourself from their grip."

— Cheryl Richardson

A Moment of Betrayal

In the silence of the early morning, you sit by the window, watching the first light of dawn spill over a quiet world. It's peaceful—yet heavy. Today carries the weight of memory. You recall that piercing moment of betrayal—a trusted friend's harsh words or a loved one's broken promise—that left your heart feeling like shattered glass. The sting of betrayal is fresh, its edges as sharp as ever.

Yet, amidst the remnants of what was, a quiet truth stirs: you don't have to carry this pain forever. There's a power within reach that doesn't require forgetting—but invites release. This is the transformative power of forgiveness.

The Freedom of Forgiveness

Forgiveness is not about excusing wrongs or pretending they didn't matter. It's about choosing to release the emotional grip those wrongs have over your life.

- It's setting down the backpack of resentment you've carried for too long.
- It's reclaiming your energy, your peace, your power.
- It's saying, "I deserve to heal, even if they never apologize."

Forgiveness doesn't mean reconciliation or that what happened was okay. It means you're choosing peace—not because they deserve it, but because you do.

It's an act of radical self-love.

The Journey of a Forgiving Heart

Learning to forgive is like learning to breathe differently. It doesn't happen in a single breath, but through conscious repetition.

Begin here:

- Acknowledge the pain. Don't minimize it. Say, "This hurt me."
- Recognize the cost. Holding onto bitterness often harms you more than the person who caused it.
- Understand your worth. You deserve a life unchained by the actions of others.

Unforgiveness often manifests as:

- Chronic stress or fatigue
- Disrupted sleep or tension in relationships
- A sense of stuckness or inability to move forward emotionally

Forgiveness offers an exit ramp from that cycle. It's not about absolution—it's about liberation.

Approach it with compassion. This journey might involve:

- Journaling

- Therapy
- Safe conversations with supportive people
- Mindfulness or prayer

Forgiveness is not a one-time act; it is a layered process that unfolds at your own pace. Every time you choose to soften instead of harden and to release instead of hold, you're making progress.

My Truth: Forgiveness as Liberation

For years, I confused forgiveness with permission. I believed forgiving meant letting someone off the hook—or worse, saying their actions didn't matter. But they did matter. They still do.

I eventually learned that forgiveness isn't about them. It's for me.

I was dragging emotional chains—anger, grief, shame—thinking they kept me safe. But all they did was keep me stuck. The day I whispered, "I want to be free," something shifted. I began writing letters I never sent. I cried. I screamed. I forgave—not because they earned it, but because I couldn't carry the pain any longer.

Forgiveness didn't erase my story; it honored it. It allowed me to step forward from my wounds into wisdom.

If you're afraid that forgiveness means forgetting, know this: your memory honors your truth. But your freedom begins the moment you choose to stop reliving the harm.

Survivor Spotlight: Maria

- Core struggle: Childhood trauma left her feeling powerless and unseen
- Turning point: Through therapy, she realized forgiveness wasn't approval—it was freedom

- Ongoing practice/tool: Letter writing and mindfulness meditation
- Where she is now: Created a support group for survivors and feels emotionally lighter

Survivor Spotlight: Damien

- Core struggle: Held onto resentment for decades after betrayal by a close friend
- Turning point: A forgiveness workshop challenged him to write a release letter
- Ongoing practice/tool: Monthly forgiveness reflections and prayer
- Where he is now: Describes forgiveness as the key that unlocked his creativity and clarity

Real Stories of Transformation

Nelson Mandela spent 27 years in prison. He had every reason to harbor hatred—but chose reconciliation. His forgiveness wasn't weakness; it was strength. It shaped a nation.

Maria, a survivor of childhood trauma, carried her pain for decades. Through therapy and her decision to forgive—not forget—she found clarity and peace. Her life opened up in ways she never imagined, all because she made peace with her past.

These stories remind us that forgiveness is not denial of suffering; it's the reclamation of life.

The Science of Forgiveness:
How Letting Go Changes Your Brain and Body

Forgiveness isn't just emotionally liberating; it's physiologically powerful. Studies in neuroscience and psychology have shown that choosing forgiveness reduces stress, strengthens emotional regulation, and even improves heart health.

When we hold onto resentment, our brain activates the stress response—particularly in the **amygdala**, responsible for fear and emotional memory. This keeps our bodies in a heightened state of tension, contributing to anxiety, sleep issues, and even chronic pain.

However, when we engage in forgiveness practices—such as reflective journaling, compassion-focused meditation, or simply setting an intention to release—we activate the **prefrontal cortex**, which governs decision-making and empathy. Over time, this shift rewires the brain's emotional response patterns.

Research from Stanford University's Forgiveness Project shows that participants who practiced forgiveness experienced lower blood pressure, reduced symptoms of depression, and improved relationships. Other studies found that forgiveness correlates with increased activity in the **anterior cingulate cortex**, which helps us resolve conflict and regulate emotional pain.

Forgiveness also lowers cortisol levels (the stress hormone) and supports the parasympathetic nervous system, which governs our rest and recovery.

In short, forgiving others doesn't mean denying your pain. It means choosing to stop reliving the injury and allowing your brain and body to begin healing. It's not only a spiritual act; it's a scientifically supported path toward mental clarity and physical relief.

More Paths to Forgiveness

Forgiveness isn't one-size-fits-all. Some find their path through prayer, others through therapy, and still others through stillness, journaling, or expressive arts. The beauty of forgiveness is that it meets you where you are and asks only for your willingness to begin.

If you've tried to forgive and still feel stuck, know this: you're not failing. You're still moving. Forgiveness is not linear; it resembles peeling an onion—one emotional layer at a time.

You might forgive someone in your mind, only to feel the pain again months later. This doesn't mean you've regressed; it means you're healing on a deeper level. Each time you revisit that wound with compassion instead of blame, you're creating new pathways to peace.

Forgiveness is not the absence of anger or sadness; it's the presence of grace. It recognizes that your healing matters more than holding on. This doesn't mean pretending to be okay; it means giving yourself permission to stop being defined by what happened.

You may also find that before you can forgive others, you must forgive yourself—for what you didn't know, for how you coped, and for not being able to change what happened. Forgiving yourself might be the most radical act of all.

Embrace This Moment

Return to the image of sitting in the early morning light. Feel the warmth on your skin. The pain is still there—but so is your power.

Ask yourself:

- What would it feel like to stop carrying this pain?
- Who might I become without the resentment?

With each breath, choose to believe that healing is possible. Let forgiveness be your way forward.

Next, we'll explore silence and reflection—two practices that help you listen deeply to your soul and nurture emotional clarity. Forgiveness clears the path. Stillness helps you hear what's next.

Try This Tool: The Release Letter

Write a letter to someone you're ready to forgive. You won't send it; this is for you.

In the letter:

- Express the hurt and its impact on you.
- Say the things you were never allowed or able to say.
- End with your intention: "I release this pain for me."

Then, tear it up, burn it safely, or bury it. Create a ritual to symbolize your freedom. This turns intention into action and helps your body process the shift.

Reflective Workbook Page: Chapter 4

Reflection Questions:

1. What is one hurt you're still carrying that might be ready to soften or release?
2. How has holding onto resentment affected your well-being—emotionally, physically, or spiritually?
3. What does forgiveness mean to you today—not as a concept, but as a lived practice?

Journal Prompts:

- Write a letter to someone you haven't forgiven—not to send, but to release your truth.
- Reflect on a time when you chose to forgive. What changed within you afterward?
- Describe a version of your life where forgiveness has made space for peace, creativity, or connection.

Affirmation:

"Forgiveness frees me to grow, heal, and create space for peace within."

Flowing Forward

As you release resentment and begin to untangle from past harm, we invite you to turn inward with stillness. In the next chapter, we'll explore the healing strength of silence and reflection—spaces where your inner wisdom can be heard most clearly.

CHAPTER 5
Embracing Silence and Reflection

"In the silence, we find ourselves."

— Unknown

A Moment of Unexpected Clarity

Imagine standing on the edge of a serene lake, the early morning mist weaving an ethereal tapestry across its surface. You're alone, the quiet enveloping you like a warm, familiar blanket. In this solitude, something unexpected happens. Clarity—that elusive understanding you'd been chasing—settles gently, like the mist itself. For the first time, you truly hear your thoughts, untainted by the chaos of daily life. This moment of peace and insight, born of silence, becomes a guiding light, illuminating paths previously obscured by noise and distraction.

Silence and Reflection: Catalysts for Self-Discovery

Silence and reflection aren't merely breaks from noise—they are invitations to delve deeper into your truth. In stillness, we uncover parts of ourselves we may have forgotten: intuition, longing, peace.

By creating intentional space for quiet reflection, you:

- Access clarity previously drowned out by distraction
- Hear your inner voice, not everyone else's
- Process emotions with compassion and curiosity
- Reclaim personal power and direction

When the world goes quiet, your inner wisdom speaks louder. Silence is not the absence of sound—it is the presence of awareness. And awareness is the birthplace of healing.

The Daily Dance of Silence

You don't have to retreat to a cabin in the woods to reap the benefits of silence. Bringing stillness into your life begins with intention—not isolation.

Start small. Try this:

- Pause for five minutes in the morning before your day begins.
- Turn off background noise while driving or folding laundry.
- End the day with a few minutes of quiet reflection instead of scrolling through your phone.

These moments are not wasted; they are sacred. With repetition, stillness becomes less awkward and more nourishing.

Mindfulness and meditation deepen this experience. These aren't mystical rituals but practical skills. When you sit with your breath:

- You train your brain to stay present
- You create space between stimulus and reaction
- You learn to observe thoughts without attaching to them

This is how self-regulation and clarity are cultivated—by giving yourself permission to be.

The Science of Stillness: How Silence Regulates the Nervous System

Moments of silence may seem passive, but they have profound physiological effects. When you sit in stillness, especially with intentional breath or mindfulness, your **parasympathetic nervous system** activates—this is your body's "rest and restore" mode.

Studies show that practices like deep breathing and quiet reflection reduce cortisol levels, improve emotional regulation, and enhance memory and creativity. Silence isn't absence—it's recalibration. With consistency, your body begins to associate quiet moments with safety and restoration rather than discomfort.

Neuroscience also shows that intentional stillness allows the **default mode network**—the brain's introspective system—to process memories, emotions, and thoughts in a way that promotes healing and emotional clarity. This isn't spiritual fluff—it's your biology learning how to breathe again.

My Truth: Facing the Fear of Silence

I used to run from silence. It felt too empty, too uncomfortable. The quiet wasn't peaceful—it was deafening. In that stillness, I feared the truth I might hear.

But I didn't realize that beneath the noise was a steady, compassionate voice—my own.

The first time I truly embraced silence, I cried. Not from sadness, but from relief. It was like meeting myself again. That voice didn't have all the answers, but it offered presence. And that presence helped me take one more step toward healing.

Later, I came to rely on silence as a place to reset, regroup, and reconnect. Even when the world felt chaotic, I found clarity in quiet—one breath, one pause, one still moment at a time.

If silence feels foreign or scary to you, I understand. But trust this: something beautiful is waiting in the quiet. You.

Silence as a Path to Self-Connection

Silence has the power to reconnect us with the most important voice we often ignore—our own.

For survivors, the world taught us to look outward for safety, approval, or validation. But silence invites us inward.

It reminds us that the wisdom we seek isn't missing—it's buried beneath the noise.

In quiet, we return home to ourselves. We meet the part of us that is still whole, still knowing, and still capable of guiding us forward.

You might begin to notice the difference between the noise that distracts you and the voice that guides you. One is urgent. The other is gentle. One pulls you outward. The other invites you inward.

Let silence become your sacred space—not because it erases pain, but because it reminds you that you are more than it.

When you build this relationship with yourself, you stop waiting for others to validate you. You begin to trust your timing, your knowing, your enoughness.

Survivor Spotlight: Rachel

- Core struggle: Overwhelmed by responsibilities and emotional noise
- Turning point: Joined a silent retreat and heard her truth for the first time
- Ongoing practice/tool: Morning journaling and silent walks
- Where she is now: Changed careers, reconnected with creativity, and practices stillness daily as a form of self-honoring

Survivor Spotlight: Tom

- Core struggle: Chronic anxiety that kept him disconnected from his body
- Turning point: Committed to five minutes of meditation daily
- Ongoing practice/tool: Mindful breathing and quiet reflection
- Where he is now: Reports reduced anxiety, increased patience, and uses silence to stay grounded in chaotic moments

Embrace the Power of Quietude

As you remember that lake or imagine your own version of it, consider this: quiet is not the opposite of healing—it's the doorway to it.

Silence helps you:

- Hear what matters
- Sift through emotional clutter
- Make space for your authentic self to breathe

Let stillness become part of your healing toolkit—not a chore, but a comfort. As we move into the next chapter, where we explore the power of community and support systems, carry silence with you as an inner sanctuary. The more you listen within, the stronger your voice becomes in the world.

Try This Tool: Five Minutes of Silence

Set a timer for five minutes. Sit in stillness—no phone, no music, no to-do list. Just breathe and notice.

Let your thoughts come and go like clouds. If your mind races, that's okay. Each time, gently return to your breath.

Even a few minutes of silence:

- Builds self-awareness
- Settles the nervous system
- Invites inner guidance

This isn't about perfection. It's about presence.

Reflective Workbook Page: Chapter 5

Reflection Questions:

1. When was the last time you truly sat in silence with yourself?
2. What thoughts or emotions tend to surface when you quiet your external world?
3. Given your current challenges, how might creating space for silence support your healing?

Journal Prompts:

- Describe a moment when silence brought unexpected clarity or comfort.
- Write about what scares—or soothes—you about being still.
- Imagine a daily practice of stillness. What would it look like? How might it change your inner world?

Affirmation:

"In silence, I reconnect with my truth and create space for peace, healing, and clarity."

Flowing Forward

After reconnecting with your inner voice in silence, you're ready to engage with the world and seek support. The next chapter will guide you in identifying and nurturing the relationships that uplift and sustain you as you continue your journey.

CHAPTER 6
The Value of Supportive Relationships

"Sometimes we just need someone to simply be there, not to fix anything, but to let us feel we are supported and not alone."

— Unknown

An Unexpected Turn of Heart

Imagine standing at a crossroads in life, feeling isolated, with the path ahead obscured by uncertainty. It's a familiar scene—where only your shadow might accompany you. Then, unexpectedly, someone steps beside you. No grand gesture, no perfect words—just presence.

That simple act of warmth or solidarity becomes a spark. Suddenly, you realize: you're not alone. This realization, simple yet profound, can transform your entire healing journey. Support doesn't have to fix you; it just needs to walk with you.

This chapter explores how supportive relationships transform isolation into connection and despair into hope.

Building Networks That Heal

Supportive relationships are more than comforting—they are essential to healing. They provide:

- Emotional regulation through co-regulation
- Reflective mirrors that help us recognize our strength
- Anchors during storms of anxiety or self-doubt
- Inspiration to persevere when motivation wanes

Psychologically, a strong support system lowers stress levels, enhances self-efficacy, and bolsters resilience. When surrounded by those who believe in your potential, it becomes easier to believe in yourself.

To cultivate healing networks:

- Practice vulnerability: Share honestly, even if it feels messy.
- Show empathy: Validate others without needing to fix them.
- Listen actively: Be present. Don't plan your response—truly hear what's being said.
- Offer consistency: Trust is built on reliability, not intensity.

Mentorship and peer support add even more depth:

- Mentors provide wisdom and lived experience
- Peer groups foster shared healing and collective strength

The Science of Connection: Why Safe Relationships Rewire the Brain

Supportive relationships activate the **oxytocin system**, promoting trust, emotional safety, and stress reduction. This "bonding hormone" not only deepens connection but also helps regulate the **amygdala**, reducing fear and emotional hypervigilance.

Being seen and valued in a safe relationship increases activity in the **prefrontal cortex**, which supports emotional regulation and problem-solving. Over time, the brain learns to expect safety instead of danger in connection—especially powerful for trauma survivors.

A study published in *Social Cognitive and Affective Neuroscience* found that holding a loved one's hand during a stressful moment significantly reduced brain activity in areas associated with pain and distress. In other words, connection helps us heal not just emotionally—but neurologically.

Every moment of safe, supportive interaction becomes a corrective experience, slowly undoing the belief that we're alone, unlovable, or too much.

My Truth: I Thought I Had to Do It Alone

For years, I believed that needing support made me weak. I prided myself on independence—even when that meant suffering in silence.

Eventually, the loneliness became unbearable. I reached out—not with a polished version of my story, but a shaky, unfiltered truth: "I don't want to feel alone anymore."

That first step—one brave conversation—changed everything. It didn't erase my pain, but it made it bearable. More importantly, it made it shared.

Support became my bridge from surviving to healing. Over time, I found people who didn't try to fix me—they simply stood with me. Some stayed. Others didn't. But each connection taught me about worthiness, reciprocity, and our shared humanity.

If you've ever felt like you had to do this alone, let me say what I wish I'd heard: Your strength is not measured by how long you go without help. It's shown by your courage to accept it.

Support and Identity: Remembering Who You Are in the Presence of Others

The people around us shape how we see ourselves. In trauma, we often internalize messages like "I'm too much," "I'm not enough," or "I have to do it all alone."

But when someone consistently shows up, validates your experience, and sees your wholeness—something within you begins to shift. The stories you've believed about yourself start to unravel. You begin to imagine that maybe, just maybe, you are lovable exactly as you are.

Supportive relationships can remind you of the truth:

- You're not a burden for having needs.
- You don't have to earn connection.
- You are allowed to take up space and be seen.

Let your circle reflect your truth—not your trauma.

When Support Disappoints: Navigating Letdowns and Boundaries

Not all support feels supportive. Sometimes we reach out with hope and are met with silence, dismissal, or even judgment. These moments can sting—especially if we've taken a big risk by being vulnerable.

Disappointment in relationships doesn't mean you were wrong to try. It means the person couldn't meet you where you are—and that's about them, not your worth.

Learning to navigate these letdowns is part of building a healthier support network. It's okay to feel grief or anger when someone lets you down. It's okay to say, "That hurt," and to re-evaluate how you engage moving forward.

Establishing boundaries doesn't close you off—it helps you stay open to the right kinds of support.

You might affirm to yourself:

- "I get to choose who walks beside me."
- "Just because they can't support me doesn't mean no one will."
- "I can honor my needs even when others don't understand them."

Remember: not everyone has the tools to support you. That doesn't mean you're unworthy of care. It means you're being called to protect your peace and seek alignment.

You are allowed to shift circles, release outdated roles, and hold space for new, nourishing connections to emerge.

Survivor Spotlight: Jasmine

- Core struggle: Felt isolated in her trauma, believing no one could understand
- Turning point: Attended a support group where she finally felt seen and heard
- Ongoing practice/tool: Weekly group check-ins and affirmations of shared strength
- Where she is now: Co-facilitates a peer group and speaks publicly about the power of shared healing

Survivor Spotlight: Marcus

- Core struggle: Grew up being taught to suppress emotions and "handle it alone"
- Turning point: Opened up to a mentor during a retreat and felt safe for the first time
- Ongoing practice/tool: Regular coffee chats with a trusted circle and journaling about what it means to receive
- Where he is now: Created a podcast focused on building healing-centered communities

Embrace and Expand Your Circle

Supportive relationships aren't about quantity—they're about authenticity.

Ask yourself:

- Who truly sees me?
- Where do I feel emotionally safe?
- Who lifts me without trying to change me?

If these people exist—nurture those bonds. If they don't, start imagining who they might be.

You deserve support that:

- Respects your story
- Honors your pace
- Believes in your becoming

And as you cultivate this circle, remember that giving support can be as healing as receiving it. Offer your presence. Share your story. Extend empathy. These actions ripple outward, creating a culture of healing wherever you go.

Try This Tool: Circle of Support Map

Draw a circle in the middle of a page and write your name inside. Then, around that circle, write the names of people who:

- Make you feel emotionally safe
- Encourage your growth
- Show up with consistency
- Inspire you with their empathy or strength

If no names come to mind, that's okay. Write down qualities you long for in a support person. This helps clarify what you seek and opens you to receive it when it appears.

Over time, you can add new names. Watch your circle grow as you begin to trust and connect more.

Reflective Workbook Page: Chapter 6

Reflection Questions:

1. Who in your life truly sees and supports you? How do they help you feel safe or empowered?
2. What fears or beliefs have kept you from asking for help in the past?
3. Given your current emotional needs, what kind of support feels most nourishing?

Journal Prompts:

- Write about a time someone supported you in a way that changed you.
- Reflect on how offering support to others has shaped your own healing journey.
- Describe the support system you dream of. What values or qualities would it center around?

Affirmation:

"I open myself to connection, knowing that support is a source of strength, not weakness."

Flowing Forward

Now that you've explored the strength found in connection, we'll shift to the equally important area of nurturing your physical and emotional health. Healing accelerates when your body and mind are treated as partners. Your next chapter focuses on building a foundation where both can thrive—together.

CHAPTER 7
Nurturing Your Body and Mind

"Your body is not an apology—it is a home."
— Sonya Renee Taylor

The Awakening

There's a moment—quiet, yet unmistakable—when you realize that healing encompasses not just your thoughts or emotions, but your body as well. Maybe it's a sharp breath during a walk, a tear during a stretch, or a sudden urge to rest after years of pushing through.

This chapter invites you to care for both body and mind—not as separate entities, but as sacred partners in your healing journey. It's time to listen inward, honor your physical vessel, and nurture your whole self back into alignment.

Your Body Remembers

For many survivors, the body becomes a battlefield—tense shoulders, tight jaws, digestive distress, chronic fatigue. Even if we don't remember everything that happened, our bodies often do. This is what somatic practitioners refer to as "the body keeping the score."

When you feel disconnected from your body, it isn't failure—it's protection. Your body was doing its best to survive. But healing invites us back into partnership with it.

Reconnection can look like:

- Placing your hand over your heart and breathing slowly
- Noticing tension and sending breath to that area
- Asking your body what it needs—rest, movement, hydration, touch
- Honoring signals like hunger, fatigue, or pain instead of overriding them

These small acts build trust with your body, whispering: "You are safe now."

My Truth: From Disconnect to Compassion

I used to view my body as a problem to solve. I ignored its signals, criticized its appearance, and pushed it beyond exhaustion. I believed rest was weakness and nourishment was indulgence.

But one day, my body forced me to stop. I woke up unable to move without pain. My mind said, "Push through," but something deeper whispered, "Listen."

I started small—stretching in the morning, taking walks without my phone, cooking meals that nurtured rather than punished me. The more I listened, the more I realized: my body wasn't betraying me; it was begging to be loved.

Healing didn't come from changing how my body looked; it came from changing how I treated it—with gentleness, curiosity, and care.

Practices to Support Your Whole Self

Healing thrives in a regulated nervous system and a resourced body. You don't need perfection—just presence.

Mindful Movement

- Yoga, dance, walking, stretching—choose what feels good
- Let movement be an act of celebration, not punishment
- Tune in to how you feel before, during, and after

Rest and Sleep

- Prioritize restorative sleep (create bedtime rituals)
- Take guilt-free naps
- Ask: "Am I tired or overwhelmed?"

Nutrition as Nourishment

- Feed yourself regularly and intuitively
- Choose foods that energize and comfort you
- Release the idea of "earning" food

Creative Expression

- Use art, music, or journaling to connect body and emotion
- Let emotions flow through your hands, voice, or breath

All these practices are doorways to embodiment—the art of coming home to yourself.

The Science of Embodiment: Why the Body Holds the Key

Our bodies are not just vessels—we're wired for survival, and trauma often bypasses logic, embedding itself in our nervous system.

Research in somatic psychology and neuroscience shows that trauma resides not only in memory but also in physical tension, posture, and disrupted physiological rhythms. This is why talk therapy alone, while incredibly powerful, may not address all trauma symptoms.

Dr. Bessel van der Kolk's work in "The Body Keeps the Score" confirms that healing from trauma requires bottom-up approaches—practices that begin in the body and influence the brain. Techniques like breathwork, yoga, and sensory tracking stimulate the vagus nerve, which governs the parasympathetic nervous system—the body's calm-down switch.

Studies show that body-based practices can:

- Reduce PTSD symptoms
- Improve emotional regulation
- Rebuild a sense of personal safety and agency

When you nurture your body through safe, gentle practices, you're not just calming stress; you're reshaping neural pathways and inviting your entire system back into balance.

Body Trust Is Rebuilt, Not Demanded

If you've spent years dissociating from your body or feeling unsafe within it, trust won't return overnight. It takes time, patience, and consistent reassurance. Rebuilding body trust means offering ongoing signals of safety.

Instead of asking your body to "get over it," begin saying:

- "I'm listening now."
- "I want to know how you feel."
- "It's okay to speak to me."

This rebuilding occurs in moments: choosing rest when you're tired instead of powering through, drinking water when you're thirsty, and moving in ways that feel like expression, not control.

Every time you listen and respond with care, you reinforce the message: "This body is mine, and I choose to honor it."

Reclaiming Joy Through the Body

Trauma often teaches the body to brace for danger. But healing invites us to remember that the body is also a source of pleasure, creativity, and joy. It's not only about regulation—it's about reclamation.

Joy might return through:

- Laughter that bubbles up from the belly
- Dancing alone in your kitchen
- The texture of warm sun on your face
- The deep satisfaction of a nourishing meal

These moments may seem small, but they are sacred. They remind your nervous system that life holds beauty, not just threat, and that your body can be trusted—not just tolerated.

Give yourself permission to feel good. Reclaiming joy is not frivolous—it is freedom.

Survivor Spotlight: Leah

- Core struggle: Chronic self-criticism and food restriction
- Turning point: Started intuitive eating therapy and learned to befriend hunger
- Ongoing practice/tool: Daily body gratitude journaling

- Where they are now: Embracing strength, softness, and self-trust through food and movement

Survivor Spotlight: Daniel

- Core struggle: Felt numb and disconnected from body sensations
- Turning point: Discovered body scan meditation in a trauma support group
- Ongoing practice/tool: 10-minute morning body scans and weekly hiking
- Where they are now: Reports stronger emotional awareness and a new sense of inner safety

Try This Tool: Gentle Body Check-In

Take five minutes to check in with your body.

- Sit quietly and scan from head to toe.
- Ask: What feels tight? What feels open? What needs attention?
- Place a hand on one area of discomfort and offer it compassion.

Even this brief pause can enhance body awareness and emotional safety.

Reflective Workbook Page: Chapter 7

Reflection Questions:

1. What messages were you taught about your body growing up?
2. In what ways have you disconnected from your body in the past?
3. What does your body need more of right now—rest, movement, or nourishment?

Journal Prompts:

- Write a letter to your body. What do you want it to know?
- Describe a moment when you felt safe, strong, or at home in your body.
- Reflect on a way you can practice body kindness this week.

Affirmation:

"I honor my body as a wise, resilient partner in my healing."

Flowing Forward

Now that you've begun tending to your inner world and physical self, we'll turn toward your outer world—creating boundaries that protect your peace and preserve your growth.

CHAPTER 8
Building Boundaries That Honor You

*"Daring to set boundaries is about having the courage
to love ourselves even when we risk disappointing others."*

— Brené Brown

The Unseen Line

Imagine a garden without a fence. Anyone can walk through, pick the flowers, or trample the soil. Without protection, that garden cannot thrive. Boundaries act as fences that safeguard the beauty within you.

As survivors, many of us were taught—implicitly or explicitly—that our "no" didn't matter. We learned that our needs were excessive and that silence kept us safe. Over time, we internalized these messages, confusing boundaries with rejection or guilt.

However, boundaries aren't barriers to love—they're invitations for healthy connections. They express: This is where I begin. This is how I honor myself.

The Science of Boundaries and the Brain

Boundaries serve not only as relational tools but also as neurological protectors. When you say no to something that disrupts your peace, you engage the prefrontal cortex—the decision-making center of the brain. Healthy boundaries signal safety to your nervous system, calming the amygdala and mitigating fight-or-flight responses.

Trauma survivors often experience heightened stress responses. Clear, consistent boundaries help reduce this over-activation and assist in rewiring the brain for safety and self-respect. Research in interpersonal neurobiology shows that individuals with strong personal boundaries are more likely to experience emotional resilience and lower anxiety.

Boundary-setting is both a means of psychological empowerment and neurological healing.

My Truth: Reclaiming My Voice

I once believed that keeping the peace meant remaining silent. I allowed others to speak over me, guilt me into saying yes, or push past my discomfort because I didn't think I had the right to say no.

One moment changed everything. A friend made a sarcastic remark that stung. Instead of brushing it off as I usually did, I paused and said, "That hurt." Her face softened, and she apologized.

That small act felt monumental.

I learned that boundaries aren't walls; they're bridges to more honest connections. Every time I honored my no, I made space for my yes to hold meaning.

Types of Boundaries and How to Set Them

Boundaries can be physical, emotional, mental, spiritual, or energetic. Start by noticing where you feel drained, violated, or resentful—these often signal a boundary is needed.

Examples:

- Physical: "I'm not comfortable hugging today."
- Emotional: "I'm not available to discuss that topic right now."
- Time: "I need 24 hours before I can provide an answer."
- Digital: "Please don't share my story without my permission."

To set a boundary:

1. Be clear and direct.
2. Use "I" statements to express your needs.
3. Stay consistent—even when it's uncomfortable.
4. Expect pushback—but don't interpret it as proof you're wrong.

Survivor Spotlight: Nina

- Core struggle: People-pleasing and emotional burnout
- Turning point: Realized she was saying yes out of fear, not desire
- Ongoing practice/tool: Uses a "pause and check-in" rule before responding
- Current status: Reports less anxiety and stronger, more authentic friendships

Survivor Spotlight: Trevor

- Core struggle: Allowing family to overstep his financial and emotional limits
- Turning point: Wrote a "boundary letter" before the holidays
- Ongoing practice/tool: Weekly self-boundary check-ins
- Current status: Feels empowered and more emotionally stable during family gatherings

Boundaries and Grief: Letting Go of Old Roles

Setting boundaries can bring relief but also grief. When you stop being the peacekeeper, the fixer, or the one who always says yes, you may lose relationships or feel guilt. This grief is valid. It's not just about others; it's also about relinquishing an identity that once kept you safe.

Perhaps you were praised for being easygoing or for prioritizing others. Maybe your worth was tied to your availability. Now, as you reclaim your right to say no, you might also mourn the version of yourself that survived by remaining silent.

Honor that grief. It signifies growth. You're not betraying who you were—you're honoring who you're becoming.

You can say:

- "I can love who I was and still choose differently."
- "I release roles that require me to shrink."
- "It's okay to mourn and still move forward."

When Boundaries Create Backlash

Sometimes, when we begin to honor our boundaries, people resist. Not because you're doing something wrong—but because the relationship was built on you remaining small. As you change, the dynamics will shift too.

You may be labeled as cold, selfish, or difficult. This is a sign your boundary is effective—not failing. It reveals which relationships honored your well-being and which benefited from your silence.

It can be disorienting when others resist your growth. But stay grounded. You are allowed to change. You are allowed to evolve. And you are allowed to choose peace over people-pleasing.

To support yourself through pushback:

- Ground yourself with affirmations: "I deserve to be heard." "I'm not responsible for other people's discomfort."
- Lean on supportive connections: Share with a friend or therapist who validates your choice.
- Recommit to your why: Remember what you're protecting— your time, peace, energy, or emotional safety.

Each time you uphold a boundary, you send your nervous system a message of safety. You demonstrate to yourself that you can be trusted.

Reframing Boundaries as Self-Love

Boundaries are not punishments—they are sacred declarations of what honors your well-being. When you set them, you teach others how to treat you—and you teach yourself that you are worthy of protection.

It's okay if it feels messy at first. It's okay to fumble, to soften, and to firm up again. Boundary work is a process of practice and repair.

You are not selfish. You are sacred.

Try This Tool: The Boundary Journal

For one week, keep a Boundary Journal. Each evening, reflect on:

- One moment you honored a boundary
- One moment you wished you had

- What your body felt in those moments
- What you want to do differently tomorrow

Use this journal to notice patterns and track your progress. You're building a muscle; the more you use it, the stronger it gets.

Bonus Tool: Boundary Role-Play

Practicing boundaries aloud can help you feel more confident and grounded in real-life situations. Try standing in front of a mirror or journaling a short script for a challenging scenario.

Step 1: Name the boundary

"I feel uncomfortable when..."

Step 2: Express your need

"What I need instead is..."

Step 3: Set the limit

"So going forward, I will..."

Practice this regularly, even if just in your mind. Speaking your boundaries, even privately, helps retrain your nervous system to feel safe being heard.

Reflective Workbook Page: Chapter 8

Reflection Questions:

1. Where in your life do you feel most drained or resentful—and what boundary might be missing?
2. What beliefs do you hold about boundaries? Which are you ready to release?
3. How might your relationships change if you began honoring your needs?

Journal Prompts:

- Write about a time you said yes when you wanted to say no. What held you back?
- Describe what it feels like in your body when someone crosses a boundary.
- Write your own boundary affirmation—a statement of what you are worthy of protecting.

Affirmation:

"I honor my needs and protect my peace. My boundaries are bridges to authentic connection."

Boundaries in Practice: Real-Life Applications

Once we learn the theory of boundaries, the next challenge is applying it in our daily lives. It can feel overwhelming to start setting limits in environments where you've historically stayed silent. Begin where it matters most: where your energy leaks or your heart tenses.

Here are three real-world examples that illustrate how boundaries come to life:

1. Workplace Boundaries

Jenna was always the "yes" person in her office. She stayed late, took on extra projects, and answered emails on weekends. When she began feeling burned out, she decided to test a small boundary: no emails after 6 p.m.

It felt scary, but after a few weeks, she noticed her sleep improved, her mood lifted, and she rediscovered joy in her work. Her coworkers adapted and even respected her more.

2. Family Boundaries

Eric's family was loving but nosy. Questions about his dating life made him dread visits. One day, he practiced a calm but firm response: "I appreciate your concern, but I'm not discussing relationships today."

It was uncomfortable initially, but they backed off. Over time, they respected his space, and their conversations deepened in healthier ways.

3. Friendship Boundaries

Lila had a friend who only reached out when she needed something. Lila realized she left every interaction feeling drained. She took a pause, stopped initiating, and when the friend reached out again, Lila gently explained her need for mutuality in the relationship.

The friendship faded—but in its place came new friendships rooted in reciprocity.

Boundaries don't always lead to harmony. Sometimes, they lead to endings. But even then, those endings create room for more aligned beginnings.

Flowing Forward

With boundaries in place, you create space for your truest self to thrive. In the next chapter, we'll explore how to move beyond emotional survival and begin cultivating a life defined not by what hurt you—but by what lights you up.

CHAPTER 9
Cultivating Gratitude

"Gratitude turns what we have into enough."

— Aesop

The Sunrise of Gratitude

Imagine awakening one morning, your eyes adjusting as the first rays of sunlight filter gently through your curtains. This dawn feels different. As you sit down to breakfast, you realize the weight of past pain feels a bit lighter. The shift wasn't dramatic—just a quiet moment of appreciation for the warmth of your tea or the memory of a shared laugh the day before. Subtle yet powerful, gratitude has entered your awareness.

That moment, like a sunrise, gently illuminates what was hidden: joy, beauty, and hope. This is the essence of gratitude—it doesn't deny pain; it simply reminds you that pain doesn't have to be the only thing you carry.

The Science of Gratitude and the Brain

Gratitude isn't just a mood booster—it reshapes the brain. Neuroscientific studies show that regular gratitude practices activate the brain's reward pathways, including the hypothalamus and the ventral tegmental area, which are linked to dopamine release—the "feel-good" neurotransmitter.

In a study from the University of California, participants who engaged in daily gratitude journaling showed increased activity in the medial prefrontal cortex, a brain region associated with empathy, decision-making, and emotional regulation. Over time, gratitude has been shown to:

- Increase gray matter volume in areas linked to positive emotion
- Reduce symptoms of depression and anxiety
- Improve sleep and heart health
- Rewire the brain toward a more optimistic and resilient outlook

By consistently focusing on the positive, you literally reshape your neural pathways—training your brain to find hope even in hardship. Cultivating gratitude isn't just about feeling better; it's about becoming neurologically equipped to thrive.

The Transformative Power of Gratitude

Gratitude is more than a feel-good idea; it's a transformative tool rooted in neuroscience and psychology. It helps rewire your brain toward positivity and resilience by directing your attention to what is working rather than what is lacking.

Practicing gratitude:

- Shifts focus from pain to possibility
- Reduces stress and anxiety
- Enhances emotional resilience
- Increases life satisfaction and optimism
- Deepens connections with others

When you make gratitude a daily practice, you cultivate an internal landscape capable of thriving, not just surviving.

Steps to Cultivate Daily Gratitude

Gratitude flourishes best in everyday moments. Here are a few ways to nurture it:

- Start small. Jot down three things you're grateful for each day—big or small.
- Use your senses. Pause to savor a scent, a color, or a flavor. Name the experience.
- Share it. Say thank you—out loud, in a note, or through a gesture.
- Make it visible. Create a gratitude jar or a visual board of things that inspire you.

Practicing daily gratitude doesn't mean pretending everything is fine. It means giving your brain a new pattern to follow—one that includes hope, joy, and perspective.

My Truth: One Honest Line

For a long time, gratitude felt like a performance. I said the words, but they were hollow. Then one day, I wrote: "Today, I'm grateful I got out of bed." That was it. It wasn't fancy, but it was honest. And that honesty cracked the door open.

From there, I began to notice little things: a friend's smile, the softness of my blanket, the quiet strength it took to keep going. Gratitude didn't erase my grief, but it did remind me I still had things worth holding onto.

If you've ever felt like you had nothing to be grateful for, I invite you to start with what is true, not what is expected. That one line could become your lifeline.

Survivor Spotlight: Miles

- Core struggle: Felt emotionally numb after childhood trauma
- Turning point: Began listing three things he was grateful for before bed
- Ongoing practice/tool: Weekly gratitude letters to people in his life (sent or unsent)
- Where they are now: Reports more emotional connection, deeper friendships, and improved sleep

Survivor Spotlight: Anika

- Core struggle: Constantly compared herself to others and felt "not enough"
- Turning point: Created a visual gratitude collage to highlight her unique strengths and moments of joy
- Ongoing practice/tool: Morning gratitude affirmations and journaling
- Where they are now: Experiences greater self-worth and appreciation for the small wins

Stories of Gratitude's Impact

Ella was drowning in grief after losing her partner. A counselor suggested writing a daily gratitude list. At first, she resisted. What could she possibly be grateful for? But slowly, her lists transformed: "I heard my niece laugh today. The soup was warm. I made it through another night." Over time, those small things formed a bridge—not away from her grief, but through it.

Oprah Winfrey credits her daily gratitude journal as a key to her personal and professional success. It taught her to see abundance where others saw scarcity and helped her remain grounded amidst immense responsibility. Her practice shows us that no one is too successful to need gratitude.

Rekindle Joy with Each Dawn

Return to your own morning—to the light that found you in stillness. Gratitude is not about denying hardship; it is about choosing to also notice the beauty tucked into the folds of everyday life. With practice, this noticing becomes second nature.

Let gratitude guide your perspective, infuse your words, and shape your day. The more you invite it in, the more space it creates for healing, connection, and joy.

Now, as we shift into the practice of setting intentional goals, let gratitude be the lens that clarifies what matters most. It makes it easier to know what to move toward—because it helps you recognize what already feels good.

Try This Tool: Gratitude Snapshot

Each day, take a photo of something that makes you feel grateful—a favorite meal, a beautiful tree, a cozy moment. Save them in a "Gratitude Album" on your phone or print them into a journal. At the end of each week, revisit the images. This visual practice trains your brain to seek out joy and beauty, reinforcing your gratitude habit in a tangible, creative way.

Bonus Tool: The Gratitude Reset

If you're in a tough moment or feeling disconnected from gratitude, try this reset:

1. Pause and take three deep breaths.
2. Say out loud: "Right now, I'm safe. Right now, I'm breathing. Right now, I'm here."
3. Close your eyes and name one thing—just one—that feels supportive, comforting, or steady. It might be your blanket, a tree outside your window, or a memory.
4. Write it down and add: "This is enough for today."

This tool grounds you in the present and reminds your nervous system that it's okay to find something good—even in the midst of hardship.

Gratitude in Community

While gratitude often starts as a personal practice, it becomes even more powerful when shared. Expressing gratitude in your relationships creates emotional safety and strengthens trust. A simple "thank you" can affirm someone's worth and presence in your life, building deeper connection.

You can practice communal gratitude by:

- Sharing one thing you're thankful for in conversations
- Starting family meals or support group meetings with a gratitude round
- Writing short gratitude notes or texts to people who uplift you

When gratitude is woven into your interactions, it shifts the emotional climate around you. It helps others feel seen—and reminds you that you're part of something larger than your pain.

Reflective Workbook Page: Chapter 9

Reflection Questions:

1. What small moment brought you unexpected joy today?
2. How does shifting into gratitude impact how you respond to stress or hardship?
3. Given your current challenges, what aspect of your life might be easier to appreciate with a new perspective?

Journal Prompts:

- Write a list of five things you're grateful for and why they matter to you.
- Describe how your body feels when you focus on gratitude instead of fear or worry.
- Reflect on someone who made a lasting impact in your life. Write them a letter of thanks—even if you never send it.

Affirmation:

"Gratitude opens my heart, anchors me in the present, and reminds me of all that is good."

Flowing Forward

Gratitude clears the lens. Now that you can see more clearly, let's talk about what you want to create next. In the following chapter, you'll explore setting intentional goals that align with who you are becoming—because clarity, when paired with action, becomes transformation.

CHAPTER 10
Setting Intentional Goals

"The future depends on what you do today."

— Mahatma Gandhi

The Power of Unexpected Achievement

Think back to a moment when your efforts yielded unexpected results—perhaps when your only aim was consistency, and success surprised you. Maybe you were simply going to the gym to stay active, and suddenly found yourself crossing a finish line you never imagined you'd reach. These experiences demonstrate the quiet yet remarkable power of intentional effort. They remind us that progress often unfolds not through grand gestures, but through small, consistent steps rooted in purpose.

Unlike vague hopes or pressure-fueled obligations, intentional goals invite alignment between your heart and your actions. When your daily choices reflect your values, life becomes not only more meaningful but also more achievable.

Intentionality as a Catalyst for Fulfillment

Intentional goal setting transcends merely writing down a to-do list—it's an act of self-respect. It affirms: I matter. My growth matters. My joy matters.

Setting goals with intention allows you to:

- Align your energy with your core values
- Move beyond trauma-driven patterns and choose growth
- Anchor yourself in daily purpose
- Visualize outcomes and build toward them with clarity

This process transforms your future from an abstract wish into an active creation. It helps you reframe obstacles as opportunities and progress as personal power.

The Science of Goal Setting and Motivation

Research in psychology and neuroscience confirms what you may already sense: setting goals activates the brain. When you establish a meaningful intention, your brain's reward centers, particularly the ventral striatum and prefrontal cortex, become engaged. These areas help regulate focus, motivation, and decision-making.

Dr. Gail Matthews, a psychology professor at Dominican University, found that individuals who write down their goals and share them with a supportive person are 76% more likely to achieve them. That's not just willpower—that's brainpower guided by structure and support.

Intentional goals reduce mental clutter and enhance emotional regulation. When trauma is part of your story, goals create a new narrative—one where you are the active agent, not a passive survivor. Each step you take affirms your sense of autonomy and direction.

So if you've ever wondered whether your goals are working behind the scenes, the answer is: yes. Every aligned intention is reshaping your neural pathways for clarity, motivation, and hope.

Charting Your Path and Building Momentum

Authenticity and reflection are the starting points. Ask yourself:

- What truly matters to me now?
- What do I want to experience, not just accomplish?
- Given my healing journey, what feels like growth today—not just in the long run?

Utilize the SMART framework to shape your goals:

- Specific – What exactly do I want to accomplish?
- Measurable – How will I know when I've succeeded?
- Achievable – Is it realistic given my current situation?
- Relevant – Does it align with my values and healing?

- Time-bound – When do I want to see movement or completion?

Daily practices also play a role:

- Revisit your goals each morning with intention.
- Reflect weekly—what's working, what needs adjusting?
- Celebrate small wins. They are significant.

My Truth: From Checking Boxes to Choosing Myself

For years, I made lists of what I thought I "should" do—get fit, be productive, prove I was okay. But nothing truly changed until I asked myself: What do I actually want?

One of my first intentional goals was simple: walk every morning—not to lose weight, but to hear my thoughts, feel my breath, and greet the day with presence. That goal transformed more than just my body; it shifted how I perceived myself. I wasn't pushing anymore—I was partnering with myself. And that built trust. One step, one morning, one honest goal at a time.

If you've ever set a goal only to abandon it out of overwhelm or self-doubt, remember this: it's not about how many times you restart—it's about your willingness to try again with love.

Stories of Triumph Through Intention

Clara once felt completely stuck. Life after trauma felt like survival, not living. So she chose one goal: drink a full glass of water before checking her phone. That decision reminded her she could care for herself. She added one walk, one journal page, one call to a friend. Slowly, her days began to reflect her worth. Her confidence grew—not from perfection but from persistent self-love.

Elon Musk, while a public figure with very different challenges, exemplifies how clear, intentional goals reshape reality. His ambitious vision and detailed roadmaps illustrate how relentless intentionality can disrupt entire industries. Whether your goal is to heal or launch rockets, the principle remains the same: clarity + action = transformation.

Survivor Spotlight: James

- Core struggle: Constantly started and abandoned projects due to self-doubt
- Turning point: Created a visual goal tracker with tiny, non-pressuring checkboxes
- Ongoing practice/tool: Breaks down goals into laughably small steps—then celebrates each one
- Where they are now: Recently completed a certificate course that once felt impossible

Survivor Spotlight: Lani

- Core struggle: Afraid to commit to goals out of fear of disappointment
- Turning point: Shifted focus from "finish it perfectly" to "show up honestly"
- Ongoing practice/tool: Sets 30-day intentions instead of rigid goals
- Where they are now: Launching a small online business rooted in her passions and healing journey

Try This Tool: One Goal, One Step

Choose one goal—big or small—and break it down into a single next step.

- Write that step on a sticky note or in your journal.
- Take the step today—even if it's tiny.
- Revisit your step tomorrow.

Momentum grows from micro-actions. Each intentional step affirms your belief in yourself and your path.

Reflective Workbook Page: Chapter 10

Reflection Questions:

1. What is one goal you've set that felt deeply personal and meaningful to you?
2. How do your current goals align with the life you want to create?
3. Given your current challenges, what type of structure or support feels most nourishing?

Journal Prompts:

- Write about a time you reached a goal that surprised you. What did you learn from it?
- List three goals you'd like to set this year. Describe why each one matters.
- Imagine your life one year from now. What intentional steps helped you get there?

Affirmation:

"With each intention I set, I align my life with purpose, possibility, and progress."

Bonus Tool: The "Why Map"

- Before setting your next goal, pause to create a "Why Map."
- Step 1: Write down the goal you're considering.
- Step 2: Ask yourself: Why does this matter to me?
- Step 3: Ask again: And why does *that* matter?
- Step 4: Repeat until you uncover a core value or deep personal truth.

This process connects your goal to your internal compass—not just external pressure. It transforms obligation into inspiration.

Overcoming Common Goal-Setting Struggles

While setting intentional goals is empowering, it's not always easy. Many survivors face internal barriers that make goal-setting feel intimidating, even paralyzing. You may fear failure, worry you won't follow through, or feel uncertain about what you're allowed to want.

Here are a few common emotional blocks—and gentle ways to navigate them:

- Fear of failure: Remind yourself that goals are experiments, not tests. If something doesn't work, it's feedback—not a verdict.
- Perfectionism: Focus on progress, not perfection. Ask, "What's one step I can feel proud of today?"
- Shame or self-doubt: Choose goals rooted in self-kindness. Healing is a worthy goal. So is rest. So is joy.
- Overwhelm: Break goals down until they feel laughably small. If your goal is to journal, maybe your first step is just opening the notebook.

Your goals don't need to impress anyone. They just need to reflect your truth and support your growth. Small, self-honoring goals pursued consistently change everything.

Flowing Forward

You've begun shaping your life through conscious, meaningful goals. But transformation doesn't stop at vision—it grows with reflection. In the next chapter, we'll explore how acknowledging your progress becomes a catalyst for greater self-trust, insight, and motivation.

CHAPTER 11
Building Resilience

"You may have to fight a battle more than once to win it."
— Margaret Thatcher

Rising from the Ashes

Picture a vast forest after a wildfire—charred, quiet, seemingly lifeless. But below the surface, life is stirring. Tiny green shoots push through the ash. Roots run deep. The ecosystem begins to regenerate. This is the nature of resilience. It's not about avoiding fire—it's about what rises after.

You, too, have walked through fire—loss, betrayal, trauma—and emerged stronger. Just like the forest, you may have been quietly regrowing in ways unseen. Resilience is the life that stirs beneath the ashes; it's the part of you that continues to reach out, even in darkness.

The Essential Nature of Resilience

Resilience is not about never falling; it's about finding your way back up each time. It's the capacity to adapt and recover in the face of life's inevitable storms.

Resilience empowers you to:

- Bounce back from setbacks
- Find meaning in adversity
- Stay rooted in your values through change
- Choose courage in uncertainty
- Trust in your ability to rebuild, even after destruction

The Science of Resilience

Resilience is not solely emotional—it's also biological. Your brain and body are designed to adapt. The prefrontal cortex strengthens with thoughtful coping, while the amygdala, which signals fear, calms with repeated exposure to safety. The HPA axis, responsible for managing stress, becomes more balanced as you learn regulation tools.

Researchers at the University of Pennsylvania discovered that individuals who practiced daily gratitude, reflection, and goal-setting exhibited higher emotional resilience and lower stress markers. Every time you choose to reflect, connect, or care for yourself, you're rewiring for strength.

Everyday Resilience in Action

You might think resilience is evident in grand moments—hospital rooms, funerals, emergencies. However, it often emerges through the quiet acts of daily survival:

- Saying no when it's easier to say yes
- Trying again after disappointment
- Choosing rest instead of burnout
- Letting go of toxic relationships

- Honoring your boundaries without apology

My Truth: I Didn't Know I Was Resilient Until I Survived

There was a time when I wouldn't have described myself as "resilient." I believed that label belonged to those who didn't cry, who powered through unscathed. That wasn't me.

Now, I see it differently. Resilience was getting out of bed when I wanted to disappear. It was going to therapy, even when I felt ashamed. It was choosing to believe—however faintly—that healing was possible.

I wasn't loud. I wasn't fearless. But I kept showing up. And that, I now realize, is resilience.

Survivor Spotlight: Caleb

- **Core struggle:** Believed emotions were a weakness.
- **Turning point:** Started journaling after a breakup.
- **Ongoing tool:** Nature walks and 5-minute reflections.
- **Where they are now:** Runs a men's support circle centered around vulnerability and healing.

Survivor Spotlight: Lila

- **Core struggle:** Labeled as 'too sensitive' for most of her life.
- **Turning point:** Reframed her sensitivity as intuitive strength.
- **Ongoing tool:** Uses self-compassion meditations.
- **Where they are now:** Trains others on emotional intelligence through workshops.

Try This Tool: "I Got Through It" Journal

Each week, write about one experience that once felt overwhelming but that you navigated successfully. It could be something significant or minor.

Use these prompts:

- What happened?
- How did I respond?
- What strength did I use?
- What did I learn about myself?

Over time, this becomes a written archive of your resilience. Revisit it during tough times as a reminder of your capabilities.

Bonus Tool: Resilience Reframe Cards

Write limiting beliefs on one side of an index card and a reframed truth on the other.

Examples:

Front: "I was abandoned." | Back: "I survived. Now I choose who surrounds me."

Front: "I failed." | Back: "I learned. I adapted. I grew."

Reflective Workbook Page: Chapter 11

Reflection Questions:

1. What does resilience look like in your life today?
2. What's one situation you thought would break you—but didn't?
3. How do you care for yourself when life gets hard?

Journal Prompts:

- Write about a time you surprised yourself with your strength.
- List five qualities you've developed through adversity.
- Reflect on how your definition of strength has changed.

Affirmation:

"Every time I rise, I grow stronger. My resilience is not just survival—it's transformation."

Flowing Forward

Resilience has brought you here. Now it's time to reach forward. In the next chapter, you'll explore how to reclaim your voice, dream again, and begin shaping a life that reflects not just your survival—but your joy.

CHAPTER 12
Unleashing Your Creativity

"Creativity takes courage."

— Henri Matisse

A Surprising Canvas of Expression

It was a cold, rainy afternoon when you discovered a new form of expression—a blank canvas tucked away in a corner of a local thrift store. Something about it called to you. You brought it home, unsure of what to create. As the paintbrush moved in your hand, something deeper stirred within. Doubt faded. Words you hadn't spoken, emotions you hadn't named, suddenly had a place to land. Through each brushstroke, the weight of unspoken feelings lifted. Creativity stepped in where silence once reigned.

That spontaneous act of creation revealed something powerful: your creativity isn't a skill to be graded; it's a path to healing, discovery, and reclaiming joy.

Creativity: A Pathway to Healing

Creativity is more than making art—it's about allowing yourself to play, express, and feel without needing to explain. When we create, we:

- Release trapped emotions and give them form
- Explore our identity without fear of judgment
- Engage the brain in healing, reducing anxiety and improving mood
- Strengthen resilience by transforming pain into beauty or meaning

Engaging creatively—whether through music, writing, movement, crafts, or play—is a practice of self-connection. It opens space for authenticity and insight where logic alone cannot reach.

Research in art therapy shows that creative expression activates the parasympathetic nervous system—your body's rest-and-restore response. It lowers cortisol, reduces trauma responses, and fosters emotional regulation. Your brain, quite literally, calms when you allow yourself to create freely.

Steps to Ignite Everyday Creativity

To welcome creativity into your life, consider these invitations:

- Try something new. Join a class, follow a how-to video, or revisit a childhood hobby.
- Let go of expectations. Create without judgment or the need for it to be "good."
- Schedule creative time. Even 10 minutes a day counts.
- Use your senses. Cook a new recipe, arrange flowers, doodle in your journal.
- Create space to wonder. Take walks, explore art, or ask, "What if...?"

Creativity doesn't require a masterpiece; it needs your permission. Let it be less about outcome and more about openness. Let it surprise you.

My Truth: I Didn't Know I Needed It

I never thought of myself as creative. I believed that label belonged to "artists."

But one afternoon, I picked up a paintbrush out of boredom. It became more than an activity—it became a sanctuary. I wasn't painting a picture; I was releasing the sadness I couldn't articulate. Every color held a piece of what I hadn't yet processed.

I learned that creativity doesn't heal through perfection; it heals through presence. The more I created, the more I felt alive. If you've ever silenced your creativity, I hope you find the courage to let it speak.

Now, I carry a tiny notebook everywhere—not to capture polished poems, but to catch fleeting sparks. I experiment with new spices in cooking and rearrange furniture just to see how it feels. Little by little, I realized: creativity is not a talent; it's a way of living.

Survivor Spotlight: Mia

- **Core struggle:** Felt numb and disconnected from herself.
- **Creative outlet:** Writing late-night poems.
- **Breakthrough moment:** Realized her words gave shape to her pain.
- Where She Is Now: Published a small book of poetry and leads free journaling workshops in her community.

Survivor Spotlight: Darren

- **Core Struggle:** Carried deep shame and emotional suppression.
- Creative Outlet: Woodworking.
- Breakthrough Moment: Built a bench in memory of his father and cried for the first time in years while sanding the wood.
- Where He Is Now: Runs a men's group using hands-on creative projects to foster healing through craftsmanship.

Embrace Creativity to Liberate Joy

Think back to a rainy afternoon, or imagine one now. Let your creativity lead. It might be messy. It might not make sense. But in those moments, you're telling the world: I am here. I am feeling. I am becoming.

Let Creativity Help You:

- Access Your Voice
- Reclaim Your Imagination
- Find Joy in the Process, Not the Product
- Rebuild Your Relationship with Play

In those small creative choices, we rewire our sense of identity—not just as survivors, but as whole beings capable of wonder.

Try This Tool: The Creative Ten

Choose one creative activity from this list and try it for 10 minutes today:

- Doodle Your Mood
- Write a 3-Line Poem
- Create a Collage from Magazine Clippings
- Dance to a Favorite Song

- Sketch Something from Your Window
- Try a New Recipe
- Build Something with Your Hands
- Write a Letter You Never Send
- Take a Photo of Something Beautiful
- Make Up a Silly Story

Keep it playful. Keep it light. Let your creativity breathe.

Overcoming Creative Block

Creative expression isn't always effortless. Sometimes, the blank page stares back. Your inner critic may tell you your ideas are silly or unimportant. When creativity stalls, it doesn't mean it's gone—it just needs space and compassion to breathe again.

Here's How to Move Through Creative Block:

- **Lower the Pressure:** Instead of aiming to create something impressive, focus on creating something honest.
- **Change Your Environment:** Creativity often returns when you shift your scenery.
- **Start with Play:** Doodle nonsense, make noise, scribble—shake off the need to "produce."
- **Name the Fear:** Write down what you're afraid of (failure? judgment? wasting time?)—naming it softens its grip.

Remember, creative droughts don't mean you've failed—they mean you're human. Keep showing up. The spark always returns.

The Psychology of Creativity

Creativity isn't just artistic expression—it's a vital psychological function. Studies show that creative acts stimulate the brain's default mode network, which supports imagination, self-reflection, and future thinking. This network helps us process unresolved emotions and envision new possibilities.

Engaging in creative tasks also boosts dopamine—the brain's "feel-good" chemical—enhancing motivation, mood, and focus. According to research published in *Frontiers in Psychology*, creativity has direct ties to post-traumatic growth. Survivors who actively engage in creative practices often experience greater emotional resilience, cognitive flexibility, and hope.

Creativity helps integrate the parts of ourselves that trauma tried to fragment. It brings coherence to our story and offers a space where no permission is needed to feel, explore, or reclaim.

Creativity as Reclamation

Each time you create, you reclaim something: your voice, your space, your right to take up room in the world—not only to survive but to *express*.

For survivors of trauma, creativity becomes more than expression—it becomes liberation. It's a way of saying:

- "I am still here."
- "My story matters."
- "I get to shape what comes next."

Creativity invites you to dream beyond what you were told you could have. To rebuild your identity not as broken but as blooming. To use every brushstroke, every note, every word to say: *this is me, rising.*

Creative Courage in Everyday Life

Creativity isn't just for the canvas, the stage, or the page. It's in the choices you make each day to bring color to the ordinary, to respond to life with imagination, and to express yourself even when you're unsure how it will be received. That's courage.

Creative Courage Is:

- Wearing an outfit that reflects your personality, even if it breaks the norm.
- Writing a heartfelt message instead of playing it safe.
- Rearranging your space so it feels more like you.
- Starting a project without knowing where it will end.
- Letting yourself laugh, sing, or daydream out loud.

Every time you choose creativity, you choose visibility. You choose to be seen not only as a survivor but as someone *becoming*. This is the quiet bravery of reclaiming your spirit—and it counts.

Reflective Workbook Page: Chapter 12

Reflection Questions:

1. What does creativity mean to you, and how might it support your healing?
2. In what ways have you limited your creativity in the past?
3. What kind of creative expression feels most freeing to you today?

Journal Prompts:

- Write about a time creativity helped you through something hard.
- List five new ways you'd like to express yourself creatively.
- Describe what "creative freedom" would look and feel like in your life.

Affirmation:

"My creativity is a source of healing, freedom, and joyful self-expression."

Flowing Forward

This week, schedule a creativity date with yourself. It doesn't have to be grand—maybe just 30 minutes of uninterrupted time to explore an art form you enjoy. Choose curiosity over perfection. Let it be messy, playful, and yours.

Imagine yourself holding a brush, a pen, a recipe card, or a melody. This is your invitation to live vibrantly, to color outside the lines, and to awaken joy. The more you return to your creative voice, the louder it becomes.

In the next chapter, you'll explore how to protect the freedom creativity opens up—by setting and honoring personal boundaries.

First, let your imagination remind you of how limitless you already are.

CHAPTER 13

Redefining Boundaries

"Daring to set boundaries is about having the courage to love ourselves, even when we risk disappointing others."

— Brené Brown

The Unseen Lines

Imagine a crowded room filled with familiar faces, yet the conversations around you blur into noise, leaving you feeling both present and disconnected. You nod in agreement to a request—something you didn't want to do—because saying "no" felt impossible. That habit of saying "yes" once felt like love, like survival, but now feels like self-betrayal. This moment of discomfort becomes a mirror, reflecting the patterns that led to your inner imbalance and burnout.

The Critical Need for Boundaries

Boundaries are the invisible lines that protect your emotional, mental, and physical space. They are not walls—they are gates meant to be opened and closed with intention. When clearly defined and honored, boundaries:

- Protect your peace and personal energy.

- Foster mutual respect in relationships.
- Build emotional safety and trust.
- Prevent resentment and burnout.

Setting boundaries isn't about keeping people out—it's about letting the right things in. Healthy boundaries create clarity in your life. They allow you to say, "This is who I am. This is what I need to thrive."

Science supports the importance of boundaries. According to research published in the *Journal of Occupational Health Psychology*, individuals who maintain strong personal boundaries report lower stress levels, higher job satisfaction, and greater life balance. When you consistently prioritize your emotional and physical needs, you build psychological resilience—making it easier to navigate both daily life and deep healing.

Steps to Establish and Maintain Boundaries

To begin the process of setting boundaries, start with self-awareness:

- Notice where discomfort arises. Is it in a specific relationship, a task, or a particular time of day?
- Identify your needs. What is lacking in those moments—space, rest, recognition, safety?
- Communicate clearly. Use "I" statements like: "I feel overwhelmed when plans change last minute. I need more notice to feel prepared."

Practice consistency:

- Reinforce boundaries with gentle reminders.
- Be ready for resistance—it's natural.

- Stay grounded in your intention: protecting your well-being.

Remember: Your boundaries may evolve as you do. Periodically reflect and adjust them to align with your current reality and values.

My Truth: Boundaries as Self-Respect

For much of my life, I confused kindness with compliance. I believed saying "yes" equated to love, while saying "no" signified rejection. However, the more I neglected my needs, the more resentment and exhaustion set in. I wasn't being kind—I was abandoning myself.

The first time I said "no" without offering an apology, it felt both terrifying and liberating. That moment marked a turning point. I learned that honoring myself didn't mean I loved others less; it meant I finally included myself in the circle of care.

It wasn't just about that single moment—it was about many. The time I turned off my phone during a weekend of rest, even though others might need me. The day I walked away from a manipulative conversation. The quiet strength it took to say, "That doesn't feel good to me," allowing silence to speak louder than justification.

Every time I upheld a boundary, my nervous system exhaled. My body felt less braced for impact. My heart grew more familiar with peace.

If you've ever felt guilty for needing space or fearful of disappointing someone by honoring your limits, know this: You're not alone. Each time you advocate for your well-being, you create space for deeper, more honest connections.

Survivor Spotlight: Emma

- Core struggle: Constant people-pleasing and burnout at work.

- Boundary lesson: Realized her worth wasn't tied to over-delivering.
- Breakthrough moment: Said "no" to a weekend project without guilt.
- Where she is now: Leads boundary workshops for young professionals.

The Neuroscience of Boundaries

Your brain is wired to protect you, and boundaries are essential for that protection. Neuroscience shows that clearly defined personal boundaries reduce chronic stress by lowering the activation of the amygdala, the part of the brain responsible for detecting threats. When you say "yes" when you mean "no," your nervous system perceives it as a violation, triggering anxiety and even inflammation.

However, when you establish boundaries, your prefrontal cortex— your center of decision-making and self-awareness—activates in a way that reinforces personal agency. According to Dr. Dan Siegel, this integration between emotional regulation and logical reasoning helps create what he calls a "coherent narrative self." In other words, your brain becomes more resilient when your boundaries are clear and aligned with your truth.

Boundaries aren't just psychological—they're neurobiological acts of self-care.

Survivor Spotlight: Kai

- Core struggle: Always said "yes" in friendships to feel accepted.
- Boundary lesson: Recognized that genuine relationships honor mutual needs.
- Breakthrough moment: Chose to leave a draining friendship.

- Where they are now: Enjoying healthier, reciprocal connections.

When Boundaries Are Tested

Even the strongest boundaries can be tested—especially by those who benefited from your lack of them. It's common to feel guilt, fear, or self-doubt when you begin reinforcing new boundaries. Others might push back, question you, or accuse you of changing.

Here's what's really happening: you are growing, and growth disrupts old dynamics.

When a boundary is tested:

- Pause. Breathe. Remind yourself why you set it.
- Reaffirm your intention: not to harm others, but to protect your well-being.
- Stay anchored in your truth. You don't have to justify caring for yourself.

Every test is an invitation to deepen your self-trust. Boundaries may cost you comfort, but they gift you alignment.

Boundaries in Relationships

Boundaries are not walls between people—they are bridges of mutual respect. In healthy relationships, boundaries create:

- Emotional safety
- Clear communication
- Sustainable connection

In trauma-informed healing, boundaries help survivors unlearn people-pleasing and reclaim their autonomy. Healthy relationships will honor your limits, while unhealthy ones will resist them. The reaction of others is not a reflection of your worth; it's a reflection of your alignment with yourself.

You have a right to ask for what you need. You have a right to be heard, even if not agreed with. And you have a right to walk away when your boundaries are repeatedly ignored.

Rediscover Balance

Let's return to that crowded room. This time, imagine pausing before saying "yes." You tune in. You breathe. You speak from your truth. That moment becomes a milestone—a point of reclamation. This is the power of boundaries: they bring you home to yourself.

In the next chapter, we'll explore your legacy—the imprint you leave, shaped by the values and boundaries you live by. With a strong sense of self, you are ready to create an impact from a place of alignment, not obligation.

Try This Tool: The Boundary Script

Practice articulating a boundary out loud using this simple script: "That doesn't work for me. Here's what I need instead..."

Speak it to your mirror or write it in your journal. This helps you feel confident and clear when you need to set a limit. Boundaries feel easier when your voice feels familiar.

Reflective Workbook Page: Chapter 13

Reflection Questions:

1. In what areas of your life do you find it most difficult to set boundaries?

2. How do you feel when your boundaries are respected—and when they're not?

3. Given your current challenges, what kind of support feels most nourishing as you practice setting boundaries?

Journal Prompts:

- Write about a recent moment when you said "yes" but wished you had said "no."
- Describe what a balanced day looks like with healthy boundaries in place.
- Write a boundary-setting script for a conversation you need to have.

Affirmation:

"I honor my needs by setting boundaries that protect my peace, energy, and worth."

Flowing Forward

This week, identify one area where your boundaries feel unclear—perhaps related to time, energy, or emotional availability. Choose a single, simple boundary to experiment with. Speak it aloud or write it down. Give yourself permission to feel uncomfortable—growth often does.

As you strengthen this boundary, notice how your energy shifts. Allow this clarity to create space for more authentic connection, ease, and personal power.

Because boundaries aren't just about protection—they're about direction. They help you determine what you will carry forward and what you'll no longer allow to shape your story. In that way, boundaries serve as the blueprint for the legacy you're building.

In the next chapter, we'll explore how your values, choices, and everyday actions leave a lasting impact—and how honoring your boundaries is one of the most powerful ways to shape a meaningful legacy.

CHAPTER 14
Embracing Your Legacy

"Carve your name on hearts, not tombstones. A legacy is etched into the minds of others and the stories they share about you."

— Shannon L. Alder

Boundaries as the Foundation of Legacy

You've taken a bold step—claiming your space, honoring your needs, and learning to say "yes" and "no" with intention. This work not only restores your energy but also shapes your legacy. Every time you choose alignment over obligation and authenticity over approval, you protect yourself and define what you'll be remembered for.

Legacy isn't built on grand gestures. It's woven moment by moment through your choices, the relationships you nurture, and the boundaries you maintain. It begins with the decision to live in a way that reflects what matters most to you.

The Spark of Purpose

On a quiet day in your study, you skim through an old journal, pausing at an entry that rekindles a forgotten vision—a dream etched between the lines of past reflections. It's a defining moment as you recognize the path your life has been shaping, with connections, lessons, and contributions converging toward something greater—a legacy. This newfound sense of purpose shifts your understanding of your life's work and motivates you to consider the impact you wish to leave behind. Embracing your legacy is an empowering step that connects deeply with fulfillment and purpose.

Legacy: The Heartbeat of Impact

Legacy resonates through your actions, character, and contributions, extending beyond your immediate presence to shape the lives and the world you leave behind. Embracing your legacy infuses your daily actions with purpose, motivating you to live consciously and intentionally. As you journey through life, recognizing and embracing your legacy becomes a central theme that reinforces personal and community values, providing a compass for meaningful living.

Identifying your legacy involves reflecting on the values and ideals that matter most to you. It's about aligning your habits and choices with these values to ensure your footprint positively influences not just your life, but future generations. Your legacy may encompass:

- Acts of kindness and compassion
- Creative contributions or service
- Mentorship or guidance
- Personal empowerment and healing
- Professional or community accomplishments

Your legacy is uniquely yours to define and cultivate.

Steps to Embrace and Cultivate Your Legacy

To embrace your legacy, begin by reflecting deeply on what matters most—your passions, strengths, and experiences. Consider these questions:

- What core beliefs guide your decisions?
- Who has influenced your life, and how might you mirror their impact?
- Where do you feel most called to serve or contribute?

Next, translate these insights into actionable goals. Let your intentions guide you, channeling your aspirations into areas where your impact can flourish. Align these goals with your legacy vision—whether it's mentoring others, volunteering your skills, innovating in your field, or fostering meaningful relationships.

Engage consistently with your community, recognizing that legacy is often a shared journey. Collaborate, inspire, and support others to foster a collective legacy driven by shared values and pursuits. This cooperative approach amplifies your efforts and ensures that the legacy you leave is enriched by the bonds and advancements forged alongside others.

My Truth: Everyday Legacy

For a long time, I believed legacy was only for the famous or wealthy. However, I came to realize that my everyday actions—the way I showed up, listened, and cared—were already writing my legacy. It wasn't about leaving something behind, but about living something now.

I remember a specific afternoon when I held space for a friend in deep pain. I didn't offer advice; I just stayed, listened, and held their hand. Months later, they told me that moment kept them going. That simple presence—that was legacy.

Every word of kindness, every act of courage, and every truth I dared to speak became the seeds of the impact I'll leave behind.

And I want you to know: if you're here reading this, you are already shaping your legacy. With each choice to heal, to rise, and to love more deeply—you are planting roots that will extend far beyond your reach.

Science of Legacy and Purpose

Legacy isn't just philosophical—it's deeply psychological. Neuroscience shows that living with purpose activates regions of the brain associated with reward and resilience, such as the ventromedial prefrontal cortex. According to research published in the journal *Psychological Science*, individuals with a strong sense of purpose live longer, report better mental health, and exhibit lower levels of inflammation.

Purpose fuels perseverance. When your actions connect to a deeper meaning—like legacy—your brain processes adversity not as a threat, but as a challenge worth enduring. Legacy becomes a neural compass, helping you navigate stress and guiding decisions that align with your values.

Dr. Victor Strecher, a behavioral scientist, emphasizes that living with purpose changes the way your body functions: you sleep better, your immune system improves, and your risk for heart disease decreases. This makes embracing legacy not only a path to emotional fulfillment but also a choice that strengthens your body and brain.

Stories of Legacy and Impact

Nelson Mandela, whose legacy as a leader, peacemaker, and advocate for human rights continues to inspire worldwide, illustrates how enduring commitment to a cause creates ripples of change that transcend generations.

Rosa Parks embodied quiet courage. Her refusal to give up her seat sparked a movement, transforming societal norms and leaving an indelible mark on history. Her story reminds us that legacy lives in everyday decisions that uphold dignity, justice, and integrity.

These stories remind us that a legacy need not be grandiose to be meaningful. It is the authenticity, intent, and perseverance behind actions that lend power and sustainability to our legacy.

Living Your Legacy Wisely

Reflecting on your rediscovered journal entry, recognize how embracing your legacy provides a lens of purpose and clarity. Let this journey guide your actions and decisions, ensuring that as you live, you create a tapestry of influence that aligns with your core values.

To live your legacy:

- Stay connected to your "why."
- Let daily choices reflect long-term purpose.
- Speak life into others.
- Take imperfect but intentional action.

Embrace your potential to impact, transform, and inspire. Living your legacy is not about being perfect; it's about being present, purposeful, and aligned with what truly matters.

Try This Tool: Legacy List

Write down five things you want to be remembered for—not what you achieved, but how you made people feel. Then reflect: Are my daily actions aligned with this legacy? Choose one small action this week that honors the legacy you're building. Legacy isn't someday. It's now.

Survivor Spotlight: Dani

- **Core struggle:** Grew up believing her story didn't matter because she wasn't "successful."
- **Legacy lesson:** Discovered that showing up with love and encouragement was already shaping lives.
- **Breakthrough moment:** After a heartfelt conversation with a niece, Dani realized her presence had inspired healing.
- **Where she is now:** Shares her journey openly and leads support groups for women discovering their own voice.

Survivor Spotlight: Marcus

- **Core struggle:** Survived years of silence after childhood trauma and believed his story couldn't impact others.
- **Legacy lesson:** Found healing through spoken word poetry and realized his vulnerability empowered others to speak up.
- **Breakthrough moment:** Invited to speak at a school assembly, his words reached students who had never shared their pain.
- **Where he is now:** Facilitates creative healing workshops and supports youth through mentorship and storytelling.
- **Core struggle:** Grew up believing her story didn't matter because she wasn't "successful."

- **Legacy lesson:** Discovered that showing up with love and encouragement was shaping lives.
- **Breakthrough moment:** After a heartfelt conversation with her niece, Dani realized her presence had inspired healing.
- **Where she is now:** Shares her journey openly and leads support groups for women discovering their voices.

Legacy After Trauma

For many survivors, the concept of legacy can feel complex. Trauma may disrupt your sense of continuity or cloud your belief in lasting impact. But here's the truth: the very act of surviving—and choosing to rise—is legacy in motion.

Every time you rewrite a story of shame into one of strength, you shift generational patterns. Each moment you show compassion instead of repeating harm, you plant seeds of change. Your legacy doesn't require perfection; it forms through your choices to love, speak up, protect, nurture, and grow.

Legacy after trauma is sacred. It's what happens when pain no longer defines you but refines you. Let that truth guide your next step.

Visualization:
Walking Through Your Legacy Garden

Close your eyes. Picture yourself walking through a lush garden—one you've spent your life tending. Each flower, tree, and path represents a part of your journey: moments of courage, acts of kindness, hard conversations, deep laughter, and lessons learned.

As you walk, notice what's blooming. Touch the petals. Feel the warmth. You see a bench at the center. Sit down. Imagine your future self joining you, smiling. What does she say about the life you've lived? What part of this garden is she most proud of?

Take a breath. Know that this garden is always growing—with every step you take.

Reflective Workbook Page: Chapter 14

Reflection Questions:

1. What core values do you want to define your legacy?
2. Who has influenced your life in a way you want to replicate?
3. How do your current actions align with the impact you wish to leave behind?

Journal Prompts:

- Describe the legacy you hope to leave in one paragraph.
- Write a letter to your future self about the life you hope you're building.
- Reflect on a moment when someone said your actions made a difference—how did it feel?

Affirmation:

"Each day, I live with purpose, planting seeds of impact that will grow long after I'm gone."

Living Legacy in Daily Life

Legacy isn't just something you leave behind—it's something you embody each day. Whether you're mentoring someone, standing up for your values, or simply making space for joy, your actions write your story.

Here's how to make your legacy tangible:

- Start your day by asking: What impact do I want to make today?
- Keep a "Living Legacy Journal" to record small moments of meaning.
- Celebrate the ways you show up, not just what you produce.

Small steps, rooted in love and intention, ripple out farther than we often realize. Your daily choices matter. You are a legacy in motion.

Flowing Forward

This week, take time to connect with someone who has positively impacted your life. Tell them what their influence has meant to you. Then, identify one small way to pay that impact forward. Legacy doesn't require fanfare—just intentional, loving action repeated over time. Let your life be your loudest message.

CHAPTER 15
Living the Life You Love

---

*"And suddenly you know: It's time to start something new
and trust the magic of beginnings."*

— Meister Eckhart

Awakening to a New Dawn

The gentle light of dawn spills through your window, casting a warm glow that awakens you to another day. In this moment, you are not just rising from sleep but stepping into a life filled with joy and purpose. This newfound clarity is the result of a journey traveled with intention—a path from trauma, through healing, to profound transformation.

Imagine waking each day with anticipation, knowing your life resonates with the meaningful actions and connections you've cultivated. This vision paves the way for embracing a life of abundance, where each day is met with gratitude and purpose.

Celebrating Transformation

The journey from trauma to transformation is neither linear nor swift, but it powerfully exemplifies human resilience and determination. Along this path, you have acknowledged past pains, embraced the healing power of vulnerability, cultivated gratitude, and set purposeful intentions. These steps have provided the foundation necessary to create a life that reflects your truest values and aspirations.

Living a life you love requires engaging fully with the present moment, enriched by the tools and lessons acquired along the way. This journey is more than mere survival; it's about thriving in an environment you have consciously crafted—a life where fulfillment is not just a distant aspiration but an attainable reality.

Applying the Lessons and Tools

Start by reaffirming the lessons learned. Practice gratitude daily to maintain focus on the present gifts of life. Set clear, intentional goals that align with your larger vision, using mindfulness as a guide to keep you grounded. Reflect often on your progress, celebrating milestones as they occur, and refine your path as needed with each insight gained.

Acknowledge the vital role of community and relationships in this process. Engage openly with those who uplift you, offering support and receiving it in return. Remember the importance of boundaries, ensuring they are respected as you build and nurture these connections.

Allow creativity to flourish in your daily actions. Whether through art, writing, music, or innovative problem-solving, let it be a breath of fresh air that revitalizes your spirit. Use creativity as a tool to uncover new opportunities and express your authenticity.

Revisit the concept of mindset with a deeper understanding. Whenever a challenge arises, remember the shift you've made from fixed beliefs to growth. Let that transformation resonate in your decisions, reminding you that you are never stuck but always evolving.

Harness the insights of emotional intelligence to stay aligned with your inner world. Recognize your triggers, respond with intention, and invite calm when storms approach. Your emotional landscape, once overwhelming, now serves as a guidepost toward clarity and compassion.

In moments of doubt, pause. Breathe deeply. Return to your center. You've walked through fire and emerged with wisdom; use that wisdom to choose your next steps with courage and grace.

My Truth: Becoming the Author of My Life

I once believed that "living a life I loved" was reserved for those who hadn't endured trauma. Gradually, I learned that my pain didn't disqualify me—it refined me. Each time I chose joy over fear, connection over isolation, and purpose over pain, I was rewriting my life story.

Today, I wake up with gratitude—not because everything is perfect, but because I am free to live honestly, fully, and with heart. I've become the author of my own life, no longer waiting for permission to feel whole.

Science of Living Fully

Scientific studies continue to validate what many survivors discover firsthand: living with purpose and positive emotion reshapes the brain. According to positive psychology researcher Dr. Barbara Fredrickson, emotions like joy, hope, and love broaden our thought-action repertoires, building enduring resources such as resilience, social bonds, and creativity.

Neuroscientific findings show that practicing gratitude, mindfulness, and goal-setting leads to changes in the brain's reward pathways, including the prefrontal cortex and striatum. These changes enhance emotional regulation and well-being. Furthermore, living authentically and embracing one's narrative reduces stress and boosts immune function, according to research by Dr. James Pennebaker.

A 2016 study published in *The Journal of Positive Psychology* found that individuals who engage in intentional activities like savoring the present and reflecting on meaningful life events experience higher life satisfaction and a stronger sense of flourishing.

Another area of research, post-traumatic growth (PTG), suggests that many individuals who experience trauma also report positive psychological changes through purposeful reflection and personal development. These changes include deeper relationships, increased appreciation for life, and renewed spirituality—all key markers of a life fully lived.

Thriving after trauma is not only possible; it's supported by science. Consistent use of tools like gratitude, boundary setting, and creative expression builds new neurological pathways, reinforcing the inner freedom and resilience needed to live a life you truly love.

Survivor Spotlight: Ajay

- Core struggle: Carried the weight of financial failure and cultural expectations.
- Breakthrough moment: Realized that his worth was tied not to income, but to values.

- New path: Started a small social enterprise to support youth in his community.
- Where he is now: Leads workshops on entrepreneurship and emotional wellness.

Survivor Spotlight: Angela

- Core struggle: Spent decades minimizing herself to avoid conflict and maintain peace.
- Breakthrough moment: Asked herself, "What do I want?" and dared to answer.
- New path: Left a draining job, began painting, and started saying "yes" to herself.
- Where she is now: Exhibits her art and mentors women reclaiming lost dreams.

Rituals of Renewal

Living a life you love isn't just about big breakthroughs—it's about returning to yourself repeatedly. Rituals of renewal serve as gentle reminders of your worth and presence, anchoring you in the moment and realigning you when life begins to blur.

Here are a few powerful rituals to incorporate:

- **Morning Anchoring**: Start your day with three deep breaths and one affirmation.
- **Evening Reflection:** Light a candle and journal a single sentence about what brought you peace.
- **Gratitude Circle:** Share one thing you're grateful for each day with a friend or family member.
- **Nature Pause:** Step outside daily. Feel the air, look at the sky, and reconnect.

- **Movement Ritual**: Dance, stretch, or walk—not for exercise, but for joy.

These simple practices remind you that healing isn't a destination; it's a relationship with yourself that you nurture with love.

Embrace Your Journey, Live Fully

As you reflect on the new dawn each morning brings, let it symbolize the life you have cultivated—a life you love and embrace not as an end, but as an evolving journey filled with growth, joy, and purpose. Recognize your transformation as the foundation for continued exploration and fulfillment, rather than the completion of a path.

Create rituals that align with this new way of living:

- Begin each day with gratitude.
- Spend time in nature to reconnect.
- End your evenings reflecting on moments that mattered.

Make space for silence, creativity, movement, connection, and fun.

Let laughter return and simplicity become sacred. Remember: you are not behind; you are blooming right on time.

Your life is not a problem to be solved—it is a masterpiece to be lived. Step into each day as if it's a canvas, filling it with intention, love, and unapologetic joy.

Try This Tool: Joy Journal

Each day, write down one thing that brought you joy—no matter how small. A smile, a song, a deep breath, a kind word. Joy doesn't have to be grand to be real. Noticing it helps you see the life you're building. Over time, this habit strengthens your awareness of how far you've come.

Reflective Workbook Page: Chapter 15

Reflection Questions:

1. What does "living a life you love" look and feel like for you?
2. How have your tools—like gratitude, mindset, or boundaries—shaped your current reality?
3. What would it mean to thrive, not just survive, each day?

Journal Prompts:

- Describe a day in your dream life. What choices led you there?
- Write about a moment you felt most alive—what made it special?
- List ten things you're doing now that support a life you love.

Affirmation:

"I choose to live fully, freely, and with intention—each day is a reflection of the life I love."

Flowing Forward

As this book concludes, remember: your story doesn't. The life you're building is alive—still unfolding with every breath, choice, and connection.

Visualize yourself as a river—sometimes slow and meandering, other times swift and bold. The rocks along your path didn't stop you; they shaped you. Keep flowing forward and trusting the current of your own becoming.

Make space for grace. Choose curiosity over perfection. Let love, joy, and healing lead the way.

Keep going. The best parts are still being written.

CHAPTER 16
What If I'm Still Struggling?

"Healing is not about becoming the version of yourself that you imagine, but accepting the version of yourself that exists right now—and choosing to love her anyway."

— Unknown

When Healing Feels Out of Reach

There may be moments—even after reading every page—when you still feel stuck. You might wonder, "Why am I not further along?" or "Why does this still hurt?" If this resonates with you, take a deep breath. You're not broken or behind. You're simply still becoming.

Healing is not a straight road—it's winding, often looping back, with long plateaus and unexpected detours. Feeling like you're struggling doesn't mean you're not healing; it means you're human, still processing, and learning to give yourself grace.

There will be days when you question whether this work is making a difference. That's normal. Healing, unlike fixing, isn't about erasing scars—it's about learning to live in peace with them.

Progress Can Be Quiet

Sometimes healing isn't visible. It's choosing not to text someone who once made you feel small. It's walking away from conflict instead of engaging. It's putting on clean clothes, eating something nourishing, or whispering, "I matter," even when you don't fully believe it yet.

These moments are victories—tiny shifts in thought and action that may not seem significant, but they are. They are acts of reclaiming your life.

Progress can also look like:

- Saying no without guilt.
- Crying without shame.
- Taking a break instead of pushing through.
- Asking for help before the spiral begins.

Celebrate these moments; they prove you are nurturing yourself in real time.

When Triggers Resurface

Triggers can reappear when you least expect them. You may find yourself reacting to something you thought was resolved. This isn't failure; it's simply your nervous system inviting you to heal more deeply.

When this happens:

- **Pause and breathe.** Ground yourself in the present moment.
- **Name what you're feeling.** Say it out loud or write it down.
- **Remind yourself:** This feeling is real, but it is not forever.

You are not starting over; you are moving forward with greater wisdom. The wound is still healing—it just needs more attention, not judgment.

You Are Allowed to Ask for Help

Struggling doesn't mean you've done something wrong. Some chapters of healing require support, whether through therapy, support groups, prayer, coaching, or simply confiding in a trusted person—you don't have to walk this path alone.

Ask yourself: "What would feel supportive right now?" Then give yourself permission to receive it.

Asking for help is not a sign of weakness; it's an act of wisdom. It's a declaration that you're worth the support it takes to thrive.

You Are Worth Showing Up For

Even on the hardest days, the choice to keep showing up matters. It declares that, deep down, you believe you are worth healing.

You don't need to feel strong to be strong. You don't have to feel ready to take the next step or know all the answers to continue asking better questions.

All you have to do is keep going.

My Truth: Holding On Through the Darkness

There were nights I lay in bed wondering if the pain would ever leave. I read countless books, journaled until my hand hurt, and still— some days—I felt like I was drowning. But I learned that struggling is not the same as failing.

The fact that I kept waking up, even when I didn't want to, proved I hadn't given up. Eventually, the air felt lighter. The tears came less often. I laughed without guilt. I began to love my life again.

Slowly, beautifully, I became someone I was proud to know.

And I want you to understand: your stuck moments don't signify regression. They're a sacred pause, a breath, a signal from your soul urging you to be gentle and not to give up.

Science of Ongoing Healing

Scientific research shows that healing from trauma is not a linear process. According to the American Psychological Association, post-traumatic growth (PTG) often occurs alongside ongoing struggles. Experiencing ups and downs is a normal part of integration. The nervous system may require revisiting old emotions to process them more fully.

Neuroplasticity—the brain's ability to reorganize itself by forming new neural connections—means that each time you pause, reflect, or respond differently, you are reshaping your inner world. Even when progress feels invisible, your brain is working beneath the surface to establish new patterns of resilience.

Dr. Bessel van der Kolk explains in *The Body Keeps the Score* that healing requires a return to safety within the body and connection with others. These two anchors—regulation and relationship—transform healing into a relational journey, rather than just an internal one.

A study published in *Psychological Trauma: Theory, Research, Practice, and Policy* (2014) found that perceived progress in trauma recovery often lags behind actual improvements in emotional regulation and cognitive function. This disconnect highlights the necessity of self-compassion and consistent tools.

Struggling doesn't signify regression; it often indicates that integration is occurring.

Survivor Spotlight: Tasha

- **Core struggle:** Constant self-blame after trauma.
- **Breakthrough moment:** Realized her inner critic echoed the voices of others, not her own.
- **New path:** Began mirror work and affirmations.
- **Where she is now:** Speaks publicly about reclaiming identity and compassion.

Survivor Spotlight: Javier

- **Core struggle:** Repressed emotions from childhood abuse.
- **Breakthrough moment:** Cried during a meditation class and felt safe doing so.
- **New path:** Embraced breathwork and somatic therapy.
- **Where he is now:** Facilitates emotional healing workshops for men.

Try This Tool: The Gentle List

When everything feels overwhelming, create a list of three gentle actions you can take for yourself. Examples:

- Take a bath
- Text a friend
- Wrap up in a blanket and rest
- Listen to calming music

- Sit in silence for five minutes

Keep this list visible. When your mind says, "you're stuck," let your list remind you, "you're still moving."

Reflective Workbook Page: Chapter 16

Reflection Questions:

1. Where do I feel I'm still struggling, and what support feels most nourishing right now?
2. Who can I reach out to for comfort or clarity?
3. What small moment recently reminded me that I am healing?

Journal Prompts:

- Write a letter to your future self on a day she feels stuck—what does she need to hear?
- List five signs that you are making progress (even if it's slow).
- Describe how you will show up for yourself this week, even in small ways.

Affirmation:

"Even on the hardest days, I am still healing, still growing, and still worthy."

Flowing Forward

This chapter is not a detour; it's part of the journey. Some days may feel like backtracking, but every breath, every pause, and every gentle choice represents forward motion. Continue tending to your healing with compassion.

Picture yourself as a garden after a storm. The soil may be soaked, but new roots are forming beneath the surface. The sun will return, and the bloom is still ahead.

Your journey is not measured by speed but by sincerity. With every kind step, you return to yourself.

You are not alone, and you are not lost. You are still on your way.

Let the next chapter remind you that trusting yourself is not only possible—it's your birthright.

CHAPTER 17
Trusting the Guardian Within

"Your intuition is the whisper of your soul—
don't ignore it. It was born to protect you."

— Unknown

Reclaiming Inner Authority

For many survivors, the most profound betrayal wasn't just what happened to us—it was being conditioned not to trust ourselves. We second-guess our instincts, apologize for our boundaries, and question the validity of our emotions. But the truth is this: you were always wise and aware. Now, it's time to come home to the part of you that has always known what you need.

Trusting yourself is an act of radical empowerment. It is your declaration that you are no longer waiting for others to protect, validate, or decide what's best for you. You are claiming that power now. You're not only reclaiming your voice—you're rebuilding your belief in it.

The Inner Guardian

Within you lives an inner guardian—your intuition, your gut, your knowing. Perhaps you quieted it to stay safe, avoid conflict, or maintain peace. But the more we ignore it, the more lost we feel.

Start small:

- Notice when your body tightens around a "yes" you didn't mean.
- Pay attention to the rising discomfort when someone dismisses your truth.
- Feel into your "no"—even when it's inconvenient.

These are sacred signals. They belong to you. Every time you honor them, you strengthen your inner compass.

Learning to Listen

Rebuilding trust with yourself takes time, just like any relationship. Begin by asking:

- What do I feel?
- What do I need?
- Given my current challenges, what support feels most nourishing?
- What feels safe? What feels off?

Sometimes, you won't have an explanation for your feelings—and that's okay. You don't need a courtroom argument to validate your intuition. You are allowed to change your mind. You are allowed to walk away. You are allowed to protect your peace without justification.

Each time you pause to listen inward, you honor your truth—regardless of how quiet or unconventional it may seem.

Boundaries Are Self-Trust in Action

When you set a boundary, you reassure your nervous system: "I've got you now." Whether it's saying no to a draining conversation, declining an uncomfortable invitation, or leaving a relationship that no longer aligns, you are rebuilding the broken bridge between yourself and your safety.

Self-protection doesn't equate to living in fear; it means living wisely and believing in your own trustworthiness. Your boundary doesn't need validation from others; it is valid simply because it safeguards your peace.

Science of Self-Trust

Neuroscience reveals that intuition is more than just a feeling; it is deeply rooted in the communication between the brain and body. The vagus nerve, which runs from the brain to the gut, plays a crucial role in intuitive awareness. When well-regulated through practices like mindfulness and breathing, we become more attuned to our internal cues.

A 2020 study published in *Frontiers in Psychology* found that individuals who engaged in daily reflective practices and emotional regulation developed stronger interoceptive awareness—a heightened ability to sense what's happening in their bodies. This ability directly influences decision-making and self-trust.

Additionally, research from the University of Leeds indicates that intuition is a form of unconscious reasoning grounded in past experiences and emotional memory. The more you practice listening to yourself, the more accurate and empowering your intuition becomes.

In short, the science confirms what your soul already knows: your body remembers, your gut leads, and your inner guardian is real.

Survivor Spotlight: Yasmine

- **Core struggle:** Doubted every decision after years of emotional gaslighting.
- **Breakthrough moment:** Realized that her constant self-questioning was learned, not inherent.
- **New path:** Began journaling daily to reconnect with her inner voice.
- **Where she is now:** Makes decisions with clarity and leads support groups on intuitive healing.

Survivor Spotlight: Leo

- **Core struggle:** Struggled with people-pleasing rooted in childhood trauma.
- **Breakthrough moment:** Noticed how drained he felt after agreeing to things he didn't want.
- **New path:** Practiced saying "let me think about it" before responding.
- **Where he is now:** Lives by his own values and teaches teens how to honor their voices.

My Truth: Listening Inward

I spent years believing others knew better. I remained in conversations that hurt, trusted those who crossed boundaries, and ignored the pit in my stomach that urged me to leave. The ache would rise in my throat like a warning siren, but I silenced it with a smile.

The more I listened to others, the more I lost myself. I felt like a ghost walking through my own life—present, yet disconnected.

One day, after a tear-filled conversation that left me shaking, I walked into the bathroom, looked in the mirror, and whispered, "Never again." I promised to stop outsourcing my safety. I began listening inward. I journaled my feelings before acting. I sought permission from myself instead of from others. My "no" became a complete sentence. My intuition became my compass. I have never felt more powerful.

Maybe you've experienced this too—stuck in a loop of over-explaining or apologizing for honoring your truth. If so, let this be your permission to stop. Trust your body. Trust your voice. Follow your knowing.

Practices to Strengthen Inner Trust

Like any muscle, intuition strengthens with use. Try these daily practices to deepen your connection to your inner guardian:

- **Body Scan Meditation:** Spend five minutes scanning your body for tension or ease. Where do you feel "yes"? Where do you feel "no"?

- **Intuitive Journaling:** Each morning, ask yourself, "What do I need today?" and free-write whatever comes to mind.

- **Pause Before Responding:** Give yourself a breath between stimulus and response. That pause is where your truth resides.

- **Reflect on Outcomes:** When you follow your intuition, write down the results. Over time, you'll notice patterns of wisdom emerging.

These rituals build trust one choice at a time.

Try This Tool: Gut Check Pause

The next time you face a decision—big or small—pause and ask: "What does my gut say?" Don't rush. Place your hand on your heart or belly and observe how your body responds. Trust builds in quiet moments. Let this be one of them.

Reflective Workbook Page: Chapter 17

Reflection Questions:

1. What situations or people make it hardest for you to trust yourself?
2. What has your body or intuition tried to tell you recently?
3. Given your current emotional landscape, what kind of support feels most nourishing?

Journal Prompts:

- Write a letter from your future self reminding you what it feels like to trust yourself.
- Describe a time you listened to your gut—what happened?
- List five ways you can practice self-protection without guilt.

Affirmation:

"My intuition is wise. My voice is valid. I trust myself to protect myself."

Flowing Forward

You were never wrong for knowing. You were never too much for feeling. As you step into your next chapter, trust that your inner compass will never lead you astray.

Imagine yourself at the edge of a dense forest, torch in hand. The path ahead is unfamiliar, shadowed, and uncertain. Yet, with each courageous step, the light of your flame reveals just enough of the trail to keep moving forward. You don't need to see the entire path— just trust the next step, and the next, and the next.

The future you are walking toward is not built on perfection but on presence. Trusting your inner guardian repeatedly is the quiet revolution that sets you free.

You are not the person you were when this journey began. You are rooted, aware, and beautifully evolving. Trust yourself. Protect your peace. Never again question the power of your knowing.

You are your safest place to land.

The Journey Continues

"You are not a problem to be fixed. You are a story still unfolding. And you get to write the next chapter."

— Unknown

You've accomplished something remarkable. You've journeyed through the pages of this book with honesty, courage, and heart—returning to yourself through practices like journaling your truth, embracing self-compassion, and setting new boundaries. Each chapter asked you to show up differently, and you did. You've explored pain and power, vulnerability and victory, boundaries and belonging. You've dared to ask hard questions, reflect deeply, and envision a life that feels more like you.

This is not the end.

Transformation doesn't arrive with a grand finale; it reveals itself in the quiet consistency of choosing yourself, again and again. In the moments you speak your truth. In the days you rest instead of hustle. In the decision to love yourself, even when it's hard.

You may not feel "finished," and that's okay. The goal was never perfection—it was presence and awareness. It was about giving yourself permission to live as the person you were always meant to be.

Let this book be a bridge, not a destination.

You will continue to grow, grieve, laugh, stumble, and rise. But now, you'll do it with a toolbox filled with insight, a voice that believes in its own wisdom, and a heart that knows it is worthy of love and joy.

You have always been enough, and now you're beginning to believe it.

Thank you for walking this path. May your next steps be grounded in truth, guided by intuition, and lit by the light that has always lived within you.

"The journey doesn't end here. It begins again—brighter, bolder, and entirely yours."

Next Steps:
Your Transformational Path Continues

You've come so far.

Every page you've read, every truth you've considered, and every moment you've paused to reflect—all of it matters.

Healing is not a destination; it's a practice—a daily choice to return to yourself with love and courage. It's journaling your truth, using your intuition as a guide, and embracing boundaries that honor your worth. It's pausing to breathe when triggers arise and finding strength in your voice when old patterns tempt silence. These tools—your tools—are evidence of your growth and the life you are choosing to create: a path that reclaims your power, joy, and right to live a life you truly love.

The Journey of Transformation: From Cocoon to Flight

The caterpillar does not rush its transformation.
It doesn't fight the process; it simply trusts that something greater is unfolding.

For a time, it may feel trapped, unseen, or unsure of what's next. But deep inside, change is happening.

And then—one day—it emerges.
Not as the creature it once was, but as something new, something free.

Your journey is no different.

Healing is not instant; growth takes time. However, you are not meant to stay where you are.

Every moment of reflection, every act of courage, and each quiet decision to embrace yourself with grace is a thread woven into the wings of your becoming. Imagine a butterfly resting at the edge of its cocoon—still, patient, yet undeniably transformed. That's you, emerging from stillness with vibrant colors, a new rhythm, and a heart ready to soar. Each choice to release the weight of the past contributes to your transformation.

And on the other side?
A life of abundance, beauty, and flight.

You were born to soar.

About the Author

Denise is a survivor and writer who believes trauma does not define your future—it reveals your strength. Her books are the beginning of a growing journey created to walk alongside fellow survivors, offering compassion, tools, and a sense of possibility. With each word, she invites you to rediscover the greatness already within you. This is just the beginning—there's so much more ahead, and she's honored to grow with you.